THE ART OF THE
Trout Fly

THE ART OF THE
Trout Fly

Judith Dunham

PHOTOGRAPHS BY
Egmont Van Dyck

CHRONICLE BOOKS • SAN FRANCISCO

ACKNOWLEDGMENTS

Of the many people who enabled me to produce *The Art of the Trout Fly*, I am especially grateful to Jack Jensen of Chronicle Books. From the time that this book was a nascent idea to its arrival in final form, he provided invaluable encouragement and enthusiasm, for which I will always be thankful.

Darwin Atkin and John Betts gave indispensable support in the initial planning stages of the book. I am very thankful to Jack Gartside and John Betts for reading portions of the text. I also appreciate the assistance and expertise of André Puyans and Keith Barton, who helped me review and select flytying materials.

Jim Adams not only supplied information essential to completing the bibliography, but generously allowed me to delve into his vast library on fly-fishing. Masao Sakaguchi of Yokohama, Japan, facilitated the participation of Nori Tashiro and Tada Tashiro by assisting with correspondence and translation.

I am grateful for this exceptional opportunity to collaborate with Dennis Gallagher, who contributed his exquisite sense of design and impressive abilities as art director to the combining of text and images, and with Egmont Van Dyck, who brought to this book a fresh way of styling and photographing trout flies.

I feel particularly honored to have worked with all of the flytyers in this book. They graciously shared their ideas, gave of their time and believed in the value of the final goal. It is to them that *The Art of the Trout Fly* is dedicated.

Judith Dunham

Copyright © 1988 by Judith Dunham. All rights reserved. No part of this book may be reproduced in any form without written permission from the publisher.

Printed in Japan by Dai Nippon Printing Co., Ltd.

Art direction and design:
  Dennis Gallagher
Photography and photo styling:
  Egmont Van Dyck
Copyediting: Sharilyn Hovind
Set in Trump Mediaeval and
  Helvetica by Turnaround,
  Berkeley, CA

The photograph on page 8 features Robert McHaffie's Gosling, Fiery Brown and Tidal Shrimp.

Portions of George F. Grant's text on page 71 are reprinted, with permission, from Grant's *The Master Fly Weaver*, published by Champoeg Press, Portland, Oregon, 1980.

Library of Congress Cataloging-in-Publication Data:

The Art of the Trout Fly
[compiled by] Judith Dunham;
photography by Egmont Van Dyck.
p. cm.
Bibliography: p.
1. Fly tying.
2. Trout fishing.
I. Van Dyck, Egmont.
SH451.A76, 1988
688.7′912 — dc19
88-2063 CIP
ISBN 0-87701-528-7
ISBN 0-87701-474-4 (pbk.)

Distributed in Canada by:
Raincoast Books
112 East Third Avenue
Vancouver, British Columbia
V5T 1C8

10 9 8 7 6 5 4 3

Chronicle Books
San Francisco, California

Chapters

Contents

Art and Artificial
Judith Dunham

When you read the literature and look at the art devoted to fly-fishing for trout, one idyllic image of the sport prevails. The solitary angler, fly rod in hand, fishing vest filled with fly boxes, quietly pushes through the current, intently casting out a long, graceful loop of line. All of the accoutrements—rod and reel, vest and waders—enable the fly-fisher to accomplish one essential purpose: to place the fly at the end of that line in view of the trout.

Much of the fascination of this seemingly single-minded quest is that the outcome is never predictable. With each cast, the fly-fisher seeks to entice the trout from its lie by using an imitation, or artificial, that replicates or suggests the insect or other organism on which the trout naturally feeds. Rather than duplicating a specific food form, the fly may embody a quality that attracts the curiosity of the fish. If beguiled and hooked, the trout rewards the fisher with a struggle through the water, and perhaps a leap or two, before being released. If the trout refuses the fly, the angler is foiled, perhaps temporarily. Despite the potential for frustration, anticipating that moment when the trout will take the fly keeps the fly-fisher casting again and again, from year to year, stream to stream.

Although there are simpler, more expedient ways to catch fish, if that is the only goal, no other method of fishing is imbued with such finesse and artistry. In taking up fly-fishing, you enter a multifaceted sport that will provide endless sources of pleasure and stimulation. You can build custom fly rods and polish the accuracy of your casting. You can journey to famous fly-fishing streams and explore unfamiliar ones. You can find gorgeous native trout in some of the most beautiful landscapes in the world. You can cast to rising trout in your mind, far away from the river's edge, by reading the vast literature of the sport. You can also pursue what, of all these many "arts of fly-fishing," to borrow Dave Whitlock's apt term, is surely one of the highest—the art of flytying.

CELEBRATING THE ARTISTRY of the trout fly, this book recognizes forty-three talented flytyers, masters of the craft who live in the United States, northern Europe, Canada, Japan and New Zealand. Having spent many, if not most, of the years of their lives tying flies and fishing, they regard flytying as an endeavor worthy of ongoing research and invention. They share their ideas on tying and the patterns they have created by writing books and articles, teaching classes, and demonstrating their techniques. They have discovered substances never before used to tie flies and have found new tools and techniques with which to manipulate their materials.

Because flytying does not exist in isolation from other aspects of fly-fishing, many of these tyers have made important contributions to entomological knowledge and angling theory and have helped to improve the available equipment by designing fly lines and other angling paraphernalia. Supporting the conservationist values important to this sport, they argue passionately for preserving the environment not only for the use of future generations of fly-fishers, but for everyone's enjoyment and benefit. Considering the creativity that can be expressed in tying

flies, it is not surprising that René Harrop, Dave Whitlock, Darrel Martin, Tim England, Al Troth, Cal Bird and other tyers are also talented in such areas as drawing, painting and photography.

Of the many descriptions of this activity that fascinates so many people, one of the best is Tim England's characterization of flies as a form of animation. In their role as animators, flytyers manipulate the material components of a fly in order to capture and vivify certain properties of natural organisms. When determining the merging of design and materials that will best effect this transformation, tyers consider many factors, including the habits and perceptions of the trout, the behavior and life cycles of the insects they are imitating, and the qualities of the environment that all of these creatures share. The ultimate appearance and properties of the fly are measured against the responses it will hopefully provoke from the fish. Tyers also take into account the fly's performance in the air as it is cast, and in the water as it floats, sinks, drifts or is retrieved. The completed fly is static when held in the jaws of the flytying vise. When the fly is fished, its configuration of materials comes alive for the trout. Marabou on a streamer pulsates and, as Hal Janssen says, breathes in the water as the fly is retrieved through the current. Fibers of polypropylene gather light to re-create the gossamer translucency of a wing on a mayfly dun. An artificial grasshopper or minnow tied on an articulated hook undulates and wiggles in the water.

Fur and feathers, tinsel and thread, plastics and foam are to the flytyer what tubes of pigment and a bolt of unstretched canvas are to the painter. They are the essence of flytying, and flytyers are constantly stimulated by seeking out and handling the materials used in their craft. For both the veteran fly-fisher and the novice, it is enthralling to sit across the table from a flytyer as he or she winds apparently unmanageable materials around a hook that is often smaller than a standard paperclip. Dave Whitlock, Helen Shaw and Darwin Atkin spin contrasting colors of deer hair on a hook with such control that they can create patterns on the body or head of a fly without using applied color. Tim England, a master in shaping deer hair, packs it so tightly along a hook that the trimmed surface is flat and compact enough to paint with intricate markings that represent small cutthroat and rainbow trout. Robert Boyle layers transparent materials to make shrimp that give the illusion of breathing with life. And Bill Blackstone is able to turn an ordinary plastic bag into the veined wings of a stonefly. These are preeminent animators at work.

In choosing the design and materials for a fly, a tyer also decides on the very process to be followed in tying that fly. Some tyers prefer to create artificials that require minimal preparation of materials and tying steps. Lee Wulff, a longtime innovator whose flies are extremely effective fishing tools, asks to be timed as I watch him add the wings and tail to a dry fly with a preformed body. He is satisfied when the finished product, tied by holding the hook in his fingers rather than in the customary flytying vise, takes only eighteen seconds. Other tyers relish the long, meticulous building of a fly that precisely models its counterpart in nature. Bob Mead, who might be defined

11

best by Dave Whitlock's term "fly sculptor," spends up to eight hours tying his Praying Mantis, a startling re-creation of a terrestrial insect that rarely, if ever, winds up in the water as food for trout.

AS ALL OF THESE examples indicate, the realm of flytying animation has many different styles and approaches, and, like painters and sculptors, each tyer in this book has his or her personal signature. Tyers may specialize in imitating a specific insect or in employing particular techniques, or they may work toward tying the broadest possible range of flies. They may prefer to tie flies based on traditional designs or to innovate patterns, or they may choose to use natural materials or to experiment with industrial-age synthetics.

Reducing these possibilities to basic functional approaches, trout flies are either realistic or impressionistic, leaving ample territory in between for variation and synthesis. More and more modern tyers are making flies that represent as exactly as possible a specific insect at the stages in its life most important to the trout. Bill Blackstone's

sculptural stoneflies and Poul Jorgensen's intricately patterned stonefly look, in their very different ways, capable of crawling off the pages of this book. Blackstone ties not only the stonefly nymph and adult, but also the emerging insect—a stage that usually occurs on streamside rocks and trees, far out of reach of the trout. Although flytying has a practical goal and is based on scientific observation, flies such as Blackstone's are made to inspire and please their creators as much as they are to appeal to the appetites and instincts of the trout. Some are even tied not as flies to be used on the stream, but as showpieces of the tyer's interest and expertise in interpreting nature.

For many other tyers, flies designed to suggest the salient features of organisms on which trout feed, rather than to duplicate realistically these life forms, make the best fishing tools. Cal Bird's exquisitely tied impressionistic stoneflies have become recognized as two of the most effective stonefly patterns in the western United States. The mayfly sequences of René and Bonnie Harrop and Barry and Cathy Beck and the caddisflies of Dave McNeese also show that impressionistic artificials can successfully evoke the delicately unfolding stages in the life cycle of an insect.

Debate as anglers and tyers do about the efficacy of impressionism over realism, or the advantages of one material or design element over another, a given fly cannot be guaranteed to catch fish. The perfect fly does not exist and, as André Puyans reminds us, may never be tied. Seeking the ideal nevertheless, tyers are continually challenged by trying to close the gap between today's fly, which the trout took, or perhaps refused with every cast, and tomorrow's, which they believe will be more productive. Another detail to analyze and improve emerges with each day on the stream and each session at the flytying vise. Is there a feature of the grasshopper, Gary LaFontaine asks, that existing imitations fail to incorporate? What does the trout see, Chauncy Lively speculates, as a mayfly drifts into its window of vision? Every question leads to an answer that, in turn, frequently generates another question.

As each generation of tyers has met these challenges, the dictionary of patterns and materials has grown beyond what the fly-fisher at the turn of the century could have conceived of tying to the end of a line. The flytyers in this book, as well as many others who are not, occupy a unique position in relationship to the rich history of fly-fishing in this century. Knowledgeable about the past and able to take advantage of its legacies, they have lived through the decades of the most dramatic changes in the sport. They are responsible for many of these changes, not only in the myriad fly designs they have contributed, but particularly in the new materials they have found with which to invent these designs or amend existing patterns. Looking beyond the materials traditional to flytying, they have discovered limitless applications for man-made substances originally manufactured for other purposes. The many synthetics used for dubbing on flies, the furry foam from blankets, the plastic of grocery bags or shower curtains, the Styrofoam of so much of today's packaging, and strands of mylar and variegated plastic have all been exploited to make creatively designed and well-functioning flies.

Necessity has dictated some of these discoveries. Richard

Talleur, a versatile tyer who enjoys making traditional married-wing flies, has had to find substitutes for natural materials that either are no longer available or are banned from sale because they are derived from rare or protected species. Motivated by both conservation and innovation, John Betts has become one of the most ingenious tyers to make flies almost entirely of man-made substances. As the flies and dressings in this book reveal, Roman Moser, John Goddard, and Nori Tashiro and Tada Tashiro—tyers from all over the world—have found successful combinations of synthetic and natural materials.

DURING THESE DECADES of dramatic change, every area of fly-fishing has been reassessed, improved and made more accessible to the expanding audience of fly-fishers around the world. Beginning tyers can peruse catalogs with pages and pages listing hooks, feathers, furs and synthetics. For instruction they can turn to many technical publications, books and videotapes, including those by tyers in this book. There are rods made of new materials and better-engineered

fly lines and reels. All types of tackle and outdoor equipment have been modified or redesigned.

Yet, the urgency to update or invent a product can often eclipse the importance of individual achievement. For anglers outfitting themselves for the stream, it is easy to buy several Elk Hair Caddis and be unaware that the pattern was developed and popularized by Al Troth, or a selection of nymphs and overlook that their basic design is by Gary Borger, or a Soft Hackle Streamer and not know that its major champion is Jack Gartside. As George Grant said to me, referring to the many tyers working today, "Everything that is happening now becomes part of history." Constantly in the process of forming, it is a history worth noticing and preserving.

Most so-called innovations in flytying, some observers feel, are merely revisions of traditional concepts and designs. I, for one, am not convinced that this is true or that it matters—for the quest to make a more effective or more aesthetic trout fly will keep inquisitive tyers striving to sharpen their perceptions of nature, to improve existing patterns, to experiment with materials, to streamline techniques, and even to create designs that they believe are new. For the committed flytyer, there is always a question in need of an answer, always an element in need of refinement. For these reasons, the tying of flies does not occur only at the flytying vise, and the pursuit of trout not only on the stream. The challenges and pleasures of flytying and fly-fishing are lived over and over in the mind with the tools and vision of the imagination.

The Life Cycle of the Fly

BIRD'S STONEFLY

DRY

HOOK *Mustad 9671, 9672 or 79580*

SIZE *#4 to #14*

THREAD *Orange*

TAIL *Black or dark brown moose body hair, lacquered*

BODY *Orange floss*

RIB *Furnace or brown saddle hackle*

WINGS *Dark bucktail, dark elk or dark fox squirrel tail*

HACKLE *Furnace or brown saddle hackle*

ANTENNAE *Black or dark brown moose body hair*

NYMPH

HOOK *Mustad 9672, weighted*

SIZE *#4 to #10*

THREAD *Orange*

TAIL *Brown goose tied in a V*

RIB *Orange thread or floss*

BODY *Brown muskrat or equivalent*

WINGCASE *Turkey quill or dyed teal*

THORAX *Peacock herl palmered with narrow furnace or brown saddle hackle*

Calvert T. Bird

I started to tie flies as a youth in Eureka, California, by studying the flies of Jim Pray, Sam Wells and other tyers of steelhead flies. The trout flies and steelhead flies of that time were all very similar in pattern. Since then, in my approach to tying flies, I tie a fly that is suggestive of something for the trout to eat—not necessarily an exact duplication of an insect, but something that serves as a suggestion of food. The fly should imitate an insect close enough so that when a fish does see the fly, it is going to take it.

I first tied my stonefly or salmonfly in the early 1960s. I was fishing near Burney, California, and the fishing was slow. I went to a local sporting goods store where I saw several two- to five-pound trout that had been caught nearby using live salmonflies. I asked for several of the flies, put them in formaldehyde and took them home.

Knowing that the colors and forms of the flies would soon fade and shrink, I stayed up until four in the morning studying the insects. Because I was a commercial artist, it was interesting for me to analyze the coloration, shapes and silhouettes of the insects. I tied four flies and sent three to Dan Bailey in Livingston, Montana. He asked me if his tyers could start tying my pattern for his store and catalog. I was very pleased with Dan's acceptance of my fly and told him that he could use it any way he wished. For over twenty-five years, this same pattern has been one of the best standard flies used in the West.

Since I was young, I have lived where there have been fish. Even when I have gone out and failed to catch fish, I have always had an exciting time. The reason for this is the challenge of trying to outsmart a trout with a fly that I have tied. Fish can be very selective at times, and to catch and release a fish is the pleasure of this wonderful sport.

[Reno, Nevada, U.S.A.]

Mayfly Nymph,
Captive Dun, Floating
Nymph, Short Wing
Emerger, Hair Wing
Dun and 3/4 Spinner
(left to right).

René and Bonnie Harrop

For some people, flytying is a hobby. For others, it is a professional endeavor. For Bonnie and me, it is a way of life. For over twenty years, most, if not all, of our income has come from flytying. I taught myself to tie flies for my personal use when I was in my early teens. Later, after Bonnie and I were married, I tied flies part-time for several tackle shops in the area of Island Park, Idaho, through which the Henry's Fork of the Snake, one of the world's premier trout streams, flows.

It was in the late 1960s that such angling notables as Ernest Schwiebert and the late Joe Brooks began fishing and writing about the prolific hatches and huge rainbow trout that inhabited this amazing river. Meeting and fishing with these talented fishermen changed the course of our lives. The demand

PALE MORNING DUN EMERGENCE

MAYFLY NYMPH
Tied by René Harrop
HOOK *Tiemco 200*
SIZE *#16 to #20*
THREAD *Black 6/0 nylon*
TAIL *Barred wood duck flank*
RIB *Fine gold wire*
ABDOMEN AND THORAX *Yellow-olive dubbing (marabou or natural fur)*
BACK AND WINGCASE *Dark blackish brown marabou*
LEGS *Brown Hungarian partridge*

CAPTIVE DUN
Tied by Bonnie Harrop
HOOK *Tiemco 100*
SIZE *#16 to #20*
THREAD *Yellow 6/0 nylon*
NYMPHAL SHUCK *Amber marabou*
BODY *Yellow-olive dubbing*
LEGS *Brown Hungarian partridge*
TRAPPED WINGS *Mallard wing quill segments*

FLOATING NYMPH
Tied by René Harrop
HOOK *Tiemco 100*
SIZE *#16 to #20*
THREAD *Yellow 6/0 nylon*
TAIL *Barred wood duck flank*
RIB *Olive 2/0 nylon thread*
WING CLUMP *Muskrat gray dubbing*
LEGS *Brown Hungarian partridge*

SHORT WING EMERGER
Tied by Bonnie Harrop
HOOK *Tiemco 100*
SIZE *#16 to #20*
THREAD *Yellow 6/0 nylon*
TAIL *Barred wood duck flank*
RIB *Fine gold wire*
BODY *Yellow-olive dubbing*
LEGS *Brown Hungarian partridge*
WINGS *Mallard wing quill segments*

HAIR WING DUN
Tied by René Harrop
HOOK *Tiemco 100*
SIZE *#16 to #20*
THREAD *Yellow 6/0 nylon*
TAIL *Light ginger hackle barbules*
BODY *Yellow-olive dubbing*
HACKLE *Light ginger, clipped on bottom*
WING *Natural calf elk hair*

3/4 SPINNER
Tied by Bonnie Harrop
HOOK *Tiemco 100*
SIZE *#16 to #20*
THREAD *Yellow 6/0 nylon*
TAIL *Pale dun hackle barbules*
ABDOMEN *Pale olive goose biot*
THORAX *Pale olive dubbing*
WING *Pale dun hackle, clipped to length*

for flies that specifically imitated the myriad insects found on the Henry's Fork and similar streams, such as Silver Creek in Idaho and Armstrong's and Nelson's spring creeks in Montana, soon grew to the point that Bonnie began to tie flies, too. Within a year we both quit our jobs and were tying flies full-time.

In 1970 we became acquainted with Doug Swisher and Carl Richards, who came to the Henry's Fork to do research for their book, *Selective Trout*. Doug and Carl had cast aside traditional attitudes in fly design with their concept of the no-hackle fly. Meeting these two innovators opened the door of opportunity for us. Dave Whitlock was also instrumental in our development as tyers.

Our personal involvement with fishing has always been most influential in the flies we make for others. Solving problems we encounter on the stream is a flytyer's greatest challenge. Tying a fly that successfully addresses a specific angling situation can be as creatively stimulating as anything I have ever experienced. There is nothing frivolous in the way we assemble our flies. We insist that they have a counterpart in nature. Although function is the most important quality, our flies must also have cosmetic appeal to be commercially successful. We shy away from exotic materials or those in short supply in order to keep our prices at a level acceptable in today's market. Although our prices may be shocking to the casual angler, our customers demand the precision, balance and accuracy that we build into our products.

Of the many changes in flytying in the past two decades, the most alarming to us has been the gradual disappearance of the professional domestic flytyer. Slowly but surely the old masters are passing on, and few young tyers are stepping into the trade. Fly-fishing is growing very rapidly, and so is the demand for good flies. Current supplies in the United States are only adequate at best, with most of the good flies coming from overseas factories operated by importers. Most of the skilled American professionals we know have more business than they can handle, and there is a waiting list of anglers who want their flies.

The collector's market is an indication of just how far flytying and the appreciation of the craft have come. Collector plates of flies tied by famous tyers both living and dead are bringing prices into the thousands of dollars at auctions and galleries across the country. Requests for framed examples of our work have substantially cut into our regular flytying production, and we are teaching our grown daughter and son to help with aspects of our business.

Professional flytying is hard work, but it has many rewards. Bonnie and I have built our business around a way of life we would not trade for anything. Living in the heart of the finest fishing and hunting in the United States—in our case, on the banks of the Henry's Fork in St. Anthony, Idaho—is something many people only dream of doing. When our backs are tired and our eyes are burning from too many hours at the flytying vise, it is comforting to know that relief is just a long double haul away.

—*René Harrop*
[St. Anthony, Idaho, U.S.A.]

Barry and Cathy Beck

We live in Fishing Creek Valley at the tail of the Endless Mountains in Pennsylvania, a valley whose extensive history dates back to the time of the Iroquois and the earliest settlers in this part of the United States. Fishing Creek, the most dependable stream in our area, offers twenty-nine miles of all different kinds of water—there are sections that hold small brook trout and broad portions of the stream that have brown and rainbow trout.

The Hendrickson pattern relates to our favorite time of year in this region. After the winter months of heavy snow in the mountains, April means the arrival of fresh spring days, and on warm afternoons the lovely Hendricksons bring up some of the best fish in the stream. The Hendrickson also reminds us of trout lilies, wake robin and columbine, all of which are in bloom at the time of the hatch. You can hear wild turkeys in the distance and sense that nature is coming to life.

The Hendrickson (*Ephemerella subvaria*) is a "gentleman's hatch," which allows plenty of time for breakfast before fishing. The insects begin to emerge from ten in the morning until noon. First the males hatch, followed by the females, continuing until about three in the afternoon.

The Hendrickson was also one of the favorite hatches of Vincent C. Marinaro, who passed away in 1986. Over our long friendship, we fished the hatch with him in Pennsylvania and other states. He had a favorite pool on Fishing Creek, and every time we go by it, we think of him. Both Vince Marinaro and Ernest Schwiebert have been very influential on our style of tying. Our flies reflect Marinaro's research on the design of flies in relation to what the trout sees, especially the importance of the wing on an artificial and on the use of split tails. In 1972 we started to sell fly patterns designed by Marinaro, and for a number of years, Barry tied all the Schwiebert nymphs sold through William Mills & Sons of New York City, one of the historic tackle shops in the East.

Through our experiences, we have arrived at a scientific approach to tying. In spending much of our time on the water—fishing and guiding—we constantly assess what flies and ways of fishing do and do not work as we observe both the life forms of insects and the responses of the trout. Most of our flies are oriented toward imitating a specific hatch and re-creating the stages of an insect that play an important part in fly-fishing for trout. We prefer to tie imitations of an insect, rather than attractors, and want flies—such as the four stages of the Hendrickson—to look as realistic as possible in shape, size and color.

[Benton, Pennsylvania, U.S.A.]

HENDRICKSON

NYMPH
HOOK *Mustad 3906B*
SIZE *#14*
THREAD *Brown*
TAILS *Barred wood duck*
REAR BODY *Dark brown dubbing*
ABDOMEN *Light tan dubbing*
THORAX *Dark brown dubbing*
WING PAD *Black goose*
LEGS *Partridge*

EMERGER
HOOK *Mustad 94840*
SIZE *#14*
THREAD *Brown*
TAILS *Barred wood duck*
ABDOMEN AND THORAX *Dark brown dubbing*
EMERGING WING *Dark dun polypropylene yarn*
LEGS *Partridge*

DUN
HOOK *Mustad 94840*
SIZE *#14*
THREAD *Brown*
SPLIT TAILS *Dark dun microfibbets*
ABDOMEN AND THORAX *Pinkish tan dubbing*
WING *Two medium dun hen back feathers*
HACKLE *Medium blue dun*

SPINNER
HOOK *Mustad 94840*
SIZE *#14*
THREAD *Brown*
SPLIT TAILS *Dark dun microfibbets*
ABDOMEN AND THORAX *Dark reddish brown dubbing*
WING *Light grizzly*

Nymph, Emerger, Dun and Spinner (left to right).

Emerger, Nymph and Adult (clockwise from top).

Bill Blackstone

Flytying has been one of the most pleasurable activities in my life since I was a teenager. Like every flytyer who becomes involved in professional tying, I easily get caught up in what I am tying at the moment and forget the enjoyment and creativity that flytying brings to everyone.

Several years ago, I became "hooked on bugs." Sure, I knew insects by name, hatching time, location, color, size and other characteristics, but I realized how little I did know. My first goal was to try to forget conventional standard patterns and materials, and concentrate on tying realistic flies. A new world suddenly opened up to me. I began to find materials that were much more suitable for the creation of my bugs. With these new materials came new techniques and methods and, best of all, a new satisfaction in my accomplishments.

My work today, which is often what you could refer to as far-out, combines a collection of materials guaranteed to hold the onlooker's attention. The Black Stonefly is

my signature fly, which I have been developing for over a decade. Every year or so I come up with another improvement. The underbody is so simple that you might laugh when you find out how it is made. I use a shaped piece of manila file folder tied on the hook and filled with five-minute epoxy. The result eliminates elaborate techniques and gives the correct body shape every time.

I also tie traditional flies, teach flytying classes and give seminars. In addition to sharing information about new techniques and the unlimited bounty of materials available today, I encourage tyers to look closely at their subject in order to know what they are ultimately trying to create in a fly. If there is one recommendation I can give to a flytyer at any level, it is *experiment*. Let your imagination open up a new world. Look at every finished fly with suspicion, and do not discard it until you have tried to make it more than once. I guarantee that tying will take on a new dimension.

[Orange, California, U.S.A.]

BLACK STONEFLY

NYMPH

HOOK *Mustad 3665A*
SIZE *#4 to #10*
THREAD *Black*
TAIL *Goose biots*
UNDERBODY *Light card stock preformed shape and 5-minute epoxy*
BODY *Neoprene strip*
THORAX *Mohair*
LEGS *Natural turkey breast*
WING PADS AND HEAD *Precut neoprene shapes*
EYES *20-lb-test monofilament*
ANTENNAE *Stripped hackle stems*

EMERGER

HOOK *Mustad 3665A*
SIZE *#4 to #10*
THREAD *Black*
TAIL *Goose biots*
UNDERBODY *Wool yarn wrapped over 80-lb-test monofilament*
BODY *Neoprene strip*
THORAX *Mohair*
LEGS *Natural turkey breast*
WING PADS AND HEAD *Precut neoprene shapes*
WINGS *Vinyl grocery produce bag marked with lithograph ink and fine pen*
EYES *20-lb-test monofilament*
ANTENNAE *Stripped hackle stems*

ADULT

HOOK *Mustad 3665A*
SIZE *#4 to #10*
THREAD *Black*
TAIL *Goose biots*
UNDERBODY *None*
BODY *Furry foam*
THORAX *Mohair*
LEGS *Natural turkey breast*
WING PADS AND HEAD *Vinyl grocery produce bag*
WINGS *Photograph storage vinyl marked with lithograph ink and fine pen*
EYES *20-lb-test monofilament*
ANTENNAE *Stripped hackle stems*

GREEN CADDIS

LARVAE

HOOK *Mustad 3906B
or Partridge L2A
Captain Hamilton*

SIZE *#8 to #16*

THREAD *Olive or tan
Danville 6/0 or
Uni-Thread 8/0*

RIB *Fine silver wire*

BODY *Bright caddis
green Hareline
dubbing twisted with
three to six strands of
olive Krystal Flash*

THORAX *Dark hare's ear*

LEGS *Dark partridge*

PUPAE

HOOK *Mustad 3906B
or Partridge L2A
Captain Hamilton*

SIZE *#8 to #16*

THREAD *Danville 6/0
or Uni-Thread 8/0
to match body*

RIB *Fine silver wire*

BODY *Dark brown
and bright olive or
cream dubbing,
twisted with three
to six strands of
pearl Krystal Flash*

THORAX *Dark hare's ear*

WINGS *Duck quill*

LEGS *Dark partridge*

HEAD *Dark gray
ostrich*

ANTENNAE *Dark bronze
mallard*

Dave McNeese

S ince I can remember, I have been keenly interested in all animals, big and small. My summers were spent running after butterflies and various bugs, snakes and other prey. I brought caterpillars into the house, where they would find a quiet spot to spin their cocoons and pupate, and after a few weeks, a beautiful moth or butterfly would magically appear and flutter about. My mother was very patient.

I had a pet bull snake that accompanied me, wrapped contentedly around my neck, on my many outings. In a more destructive mood, my friends and I sought out bee's nests and threw rocks at them to knock them down. Daring each other to get as close as we could to a nest, we ran for our lives as the bees swarmed after us. We did not always escape without getting stung. All of these childhood adventures were my way of observing and learning about the creations of nature that fascinated me so much.

This fascination naturally carried over into aquatic insects as I watched my father take trout, cast after cast, with a Bucktail Caddis on the McKenzie River in Oregon. It wasn't long before I was fly-fishing and tying adult caddis patterns. My first attempts at making flies, at the age of six, were very crude and poorly tied, although I was very proud of them. After a few years, my understanding of how to tie a properly proportioned fly with furs and feathers greatly improved.

Catching fish was frustrating because I

Green Caddis Larvae (left) and Pupae (right).

could not figure out why they vigorously attacked my dry flies at some times, then at others failed to be interested. So I began to experiment. Looking at the contents of the stomachs of trout revealed that cutthroat and rainbow loved the caddis, but not necessarily the adult caddis. To find out where the caddis "periwinkle" pupae came from, I began to place large pieces of window screening in my favorite riffles to catch the insects drifting down the river. I then compared these collections with the stomach samplings of trout taken near the screening.

In the morning I found many green caddis pupae on the screening, and the stomach samplings also showed that fish were taking these same insects early in the day. Not all caddis pupae emerged during the evening hatch, as was commonly assumed by most modern tyers and anglers. Some caddis pupae emerged during the day, then drifted and swam about until sundown. Studying this activity further, I discovered that trout and whitefish were extremely selective about this food source, literally packing their stomachs full of pupae all day long. This activity happens not only in one river system, but in the majority of western freestone rivers I have studied.

As my next goal, I developed patterns imitating the flies that the fish were taking. Over a three-year period, I decided to fish exclusively with dry flies for one year, wet flies for the next, and nymphs for the last. This forced me to concentrate on, explore, and experiment with various techniques in casting, tying patterns, and using the movement of a pattern to realize its full potential in taking trout. Color and size of a pattern are significant, but the importance of its movement in the water should not be underemphasized.

Over the years, I have gained much knowledge about the behavior of trout and insects and about the patterns that imitate insects. For me, this knowledge came through experience. Books can be helpful, but the doing and the observing are valuable sources of information for the fly-fisher. I never think I have learned everything there is to know—it is an ongoing process.

[Salem, Oregon, U.S.A.]

Caddis Skimmer, McKenzie Caddis, Fluttering Caddis, Bucktail Caddis (left to right).

CADDIS SKIMMER
HOOK *Mustad 94840 or Partridge L2A Captain Hamilton*
SIZE *#8 to #16*
THREAD *Danville 6/0 or Uni-Thread 8/0 to match body*
RIB *Fine silver wire*
BODY *Bright olive, cream and dark brown dubbing twisted with three to six strands of pearl Krystal Flash*
WINGS *Duck quill topped with dark partridge*
THORAX *Dark hare's ear dubbing*

McKENZIE CADDIS
HOOK *Mustad 94840 or 9671 or Partridge L2A Captain Hamilton*
SIZE *#8 to #16*
THREAD *Danville 6/0 to match body*
RIB *Fine wire or twisted fluorescent floss*
BODY *Olive, tan, cinnamon brown and pale orange dubbing twisted with three to six strands of pearl Krystal Flash*
HACKLE *Natural blue dun and dark ginger, palmered*
WING *Natural dun gray deer hair with two turns of body dubbing as a collar*

FLUTTERING CADDIS
HOOK *Mustad 94840 or 9671 or Partridge L2A Captain Hamilton*
SIZE *#6 to #16*
THREAD *Danville 6/0 to match body*
BODY *Olive, tan, cinnamon brown and pale orange dubbing twisted with three to six strands of pearl Krystal Flash*
HACKLE *Natural dun or dark ginger*
WINGS *Upright dun deer hair*

BUCKTAIL CADDIS
HOOK *Mustad 94840 or 9671 or Partridge L2A Captain Hamilton*
SIZE *#6 to #16*
THREAD *Danville 6/0 to match body*
TAIL *Deer hair*
BODY *Olive, tan, cinnamon brown and pale orange dubbing twisted with three to six strands of pearl Krystal Flash*
WINGS *Dun deer hair*
HACKLE *Dun or dark ginger*

The Subsurface Fly

Robert H. Boyle

I began tying flies almost twenty-five years ago when Harry Darbee kindly gave me my first lesson, and since then I have concentrated on imitating three different invertebrates: adult dragonflies, stonefly nymphs and adults, and grass shrimp.

My style of tying is realistic. I collect and observe the living species I am seeking to imitate, and I read all about its life history and ecology. My library of books and scientific publications on natural history alone runs close to two thousand volumes. Indeed, I often become more engrossed in an organism than in the fish I seek to catch with my imitation.

I now use both natural and synthetic materials, but years ago, when I was in my dragonfly bass-bugging phase, I would only tie my imitations with natural materials that I had personally collected from animals living near the pond I was fishing. Furthermore, every ultrarealistic bug that I tied with these materials had to imitate an exact species that I captured flying around the pond. Insane, but challenging, and I caught a lot of largemouth bass.

My Grass Shrimp is patterned after *Palaemonetes pugio*, which lives in brackish waters along the Atlantic Coast and reaches a maximum length of two inches. I originally tied it for striped bass. It has also taken white perch, mackerel, bluefish and Atlantic salmon in Norway and Canada. It has even taken fish that have never seen a grass shrimp, such as rainbow trout in Colorado and smallmouth bass in New York City reservoirs.

In life, the grass shrimp is transparent, which accounts for its other common name, glass shrimp. You can look inside one and see the heart at work, a matter of great significance in the history of medical research and biology. I have seventeen live grass shrimp, including three large egg-laden females, in an aquarium near my desk. I am hoping that the eggs will hatch and that I can raise the larvae in captivity, but this is chancy business. Grass shrimp are fascinating animals. I never tire of them.

[Cold Spring, New York, U.S.A.]

GRASS SHRIMP

HOOK *Mustad wide-gap bait hook, slightly reversed, turned-up eye*

SIZE *#2 to #12*

THREAD *Transparent Dyno sewing thread*

EYES *Short length of 30- to 50-lb-test monofilament, burnt at both ends*

SHORT ANTENNAE *Polar bear hair*

LIP PLATES *Clear plastic soda straw or clear goose quill*

LONG ANTENNAE *Hog bristle*

TAIL *If used, same as lip plates*

ABDOMEN *Transparent Swannundaze*

THORAX *Transparent vinyl strip*

LEGS *Polar bear hair or ten hog bristles*

TYING CEMENT *Sally Hansen's "Hard as Nails" nail polish, to coat body*

Hugh McDowell

Ideally, for me, fly-fishing for trout is a combination of things, a sort of package deal, and just being around water with all its attendant sights and sounds and smells is a big part of it. But perhaps the biggest part is fooling the fish into taking my artificial fly—this expert who has had nothing to do all its life but sort out real flies from look-alike twigs or berries or pebbles, looking over each piece like a Dutch diamond cutter picking real gems from fakes.

But I intend to fool this fish into taking my little fly. Before I begin I like to sit on the bank and plan my strategy, listening to the river for a while, studying the myriad little currents and eddies and backwaters. If the fish are not rising, I will figure out where they are likely to be lying and what they are likely to be feeding on and decide which fly to fool them with.

I can already feel the rod flexing and see the line rolling out as, in my mind, I begin to fish the pool. I know exactly where I am going to place my fly and how I am going to present it and what is going to happen when it gets there. It all takes place in my head before I reach into my vest for my fly box, and I have usually fished the entire pool and caught that trout and its mate upstream before I actually enter the water.

I sometimes tie flies for the sheer pleasure of their creation, matching feather to feather, making hackles obey and lie just so, blending colors and tones, painting a picture with feather, fur, silk and tinsel. But as a professional guide I need flies that simply catch fish, and probably the most effective ones are impressionistic nymphs and emerger patterns. For these I like slim, shaggy bodies of rough-dubbed fur, with a rib of tinsel maybe, and a turn or two of soft, webby hackle that will move in the water to give the illusion of life. But they must be simple: I frequently need replacements in a hurry, so I need something that is uncomplicated and easy to tie quickly.

People often ask me, "How do you decide when you have reached a satisfactory level of flytying?" I do not know the answer or indeed if there is one, but you will know that you are on the right track when you find yourself opening your fly box and confidently choosing one of your own flies rather than a store-bought one.

[Ngongotaha, New Zealand]

Jack Gartside

If all the fish in the waters of the world were to disappear tomorrow, I would still continue to tie flies. I once said this to a friend to try to explain my enthusiasm for and fascination with flytying. The statement explains little, of course, but rather only hints at the limits of my enthusiasm—the implication being that there are satisfactions inherent in flytying that go beyond the mere practical use of the fly as a fish-catching device.

What are these satisfactions? From the simple to the sublime, the pleasures of flytying are many: from the simple selection of the hook around which our fancies will be fashioned to an understanding and appreciation of the tools and techniques of construction; from the sensual and tactile beauty of the materials used to the physical and aesthetic satisfactions of handiwork well done, to the workings of the imagination expressed in furs, feathers and folderol.

There is also the contemplative pleasure to be had from sharing in a tradition that puts one in touch with the ideas and experiences of others who have preceded us. To tie a Royal Wulff, for example, is to connect oneself with both the rather elaborate Victorian fancy of Tom Bosworth, Queen Victoria's coachman, who designed the original Royal Coachman, and the twentieth-century native pragmatism of Lee Wulff, who substituted more practical, durable deer hair for the fragile duck wings and exotic golden pheasant of the original design. Each connection engages the active imagination in many different ways.

But many flytyers, myself included, wish to go beyond the traditional, the accepted ways of doing things, exercise our own imaginations and tap into whatever is unique and individual in our own approaches. This leads to the area of creative design, for me the most challenging and satisfying aspect of flytying.

The choices facing the fly designer are as numerous as the satisfactions. One may choose the path of realism, in which nature

SOFT HACKLE STREAMER

HOOK *Mustad 3406*
SIZE *#2 to #6*
THREAD *Color of choice*
BODY *None*
TINSEL *One or two strands of gold or silver mylar or Flashabou*
WING *Marabou blood plume*
COLLAR *Barred mallard flank, pheasant rump, guinea or other long, soft hackle feather*

is the model and the flytyer its faithful copyist. Another may approach the problem of design in an impressionistic manner, being concerned less with replicating reality than with creating the illusion of life through the manipulation of light, color and form. Still another tyer may take the path of the behaviorist, whose design concerns center around how an insect or other food form behaves in its natural environment, and will build into the design what he believes to be attractive behavior patterns. One may also successfully combine elements of each approach. Add to these design considerations a tyer's thoughts on the perceptions of the trout and the manner in which the fly is to be fished—which greatly influence, or should influence, the design of a fly—and the challenges become even more interesting.

The Soft Hackle Streamer represents yet another approach to design—that of the minimalist. I wanted to design a practical streamer that would reduce to a minimum the details and essentials of baitfish imitation, creating the illusion of life and completeness of form through subtraction rather than addition of materials. I wanted as well a fly that would look good, fish well, and be durable and easy to tie. The result is a fly whose four material elements—hook, marabou, mylar and feather collar—work in concert with the design to achieve what I wanted.

The Soft Hackle Streamer differs in several ways from conventional streamer designs. First, there is the hook. The short shank and the wide gap of the hook ensure better

hooking of the fish and deter wing-fouling, a bothersome problem with most long-winged flies.

The wing is formed by tying a marabou feather around the hook shank rather than by tying whole feathers or clumps of fibers to the top of the hook shank. This reduces the need for bulk in the wing while creating the appearance of substance, even when the fly is wet. Reducing the bulk also results in a fly whose wing is less resistant to air and water, making it easier to cast and sink, and therefore easier to fish than most marabou streamers. Light plays freely among the fibers, further enhancing the illusion of life, and making for a more attractive fly. This method of winging also eliminates the un-natural and disturbing separation of wing and body that exists in more traditional flies. With the Soft Hackle Streamer, wing and body are one and the same, a more natural approach to baitfish imitation.

The tinsel, placed inside the wing and veiled by the marabou fibers, causes light to emanate from within the fly rather than creating unnatural glare from without that may frighten fish as often as it attracts them. The collar serves several purposes. It breaks up the solid wing color and adds a touch of realistic barring, blotching or striping, depending on the feather chosen, and it creates a bit of water resistance in front of the soft marabou fibers, helping to keep them from collapsing under the pressures of current and retrieve.

[Boston, Massachusetts, U.S.A.]

Nori Tashiro and Tada Tashiro

Flies have a strong, marvelous power, and each is meaningful as a point of contact with nature. Embodied in the fly is a message that reflects the tyer's point of view about nature. By creating an enduring fly, you convey your message to future fly-fishers. Through this language, we want to make a connection with nature and to communicate with fly-fishers in Japan and all over the world.

The real pleasure of flytying and fly-fishing is in discovering new aspects about nature. In order to create a new fly pattern, improve an existing fly or develop an effective fishing strategy, we believe it is necessary to take into account entomology, ecology and behavioral science. When we first set out to expand the acceptance of fly-fishing in Japan and to convince anglers to fish with flies rather than live bait, we started to research and identify the aquatic insects found in lakes and streams. We placed nets in streams to determine the presence and numbers of insects over time, and we analyzed the contents of the stomachs of trout. We looked at insect specimens under a microscope, and we took photographs of mayflies and caddis-flies in their various life stages, at first in an aquarium and then in the field, not only for ourselves but to share the information with other fly-fishers.

Through these investigations, we became very interested in certain mayflies hatching on the surface of the water, especially after seeing the trout eat them frantically in the evenings. The flies we invented to imitate this stage of the mayfly emphasize the position of the body hanging at an angle just beneath the surface of the water. We found that Styrofoam, used for the wingcases, was the best material for flotation and visibility.

The mayflies often emerged too fast to enable exact identification of their configurations. Using a camera and strobe that could take five pictures per second, we could clearly see the emerging insects and determine the nature of their movements in the water. We became fascinated with how and at what speed mayflies such as the *Ephemera* and *Isonychia* swam. We were surprised to find that they struggled to move faster as they tried to escape the trout and that the trout preferred the active insects over the slower ones. Employing the same photographic techniques, we recorded these battles between trout and insects.

Excellent swimmers, these mayflies bend their bodies up and down as they emerge on the surface, or as they drift above the bottom of the stream and alter their direction to reach weeds or stones. The flies we designed not only imitate the shapes of the swimming nymphs but simulate their movements in the water. Flies tied on hooks with the point down, and with lead wire wound around the elongated neck, reproduce the undulating

Ephemera Swimming Nymph, Isonychia Swimming Nymph and Ephemerella Floating Nymph (clockwise from left).

and kicking of the swimming naturals. Flies tied on hooks with the point up, and with lead wire wound around the hook shank, resemble the emerging and drifting naturals wobbling in the current. A fly-fisher can enhance the action of the artificials by jiggling the rod or changing the speed of the retrieve. We are certain that our future findings will be reflected in the creation of additional new flies.

Fly-fishing in Japan is very similar to fly-fishing in other parts of the world, although we do have some beautiful, unique trout, such as *yamame* and *iwana*, and a distinctive landscape. In the center of mainland Japan, there is a mountain range about three thousand meters high running north to south like the keel of a boat. Originating at the top of these high mountains, the rivers flow as cataracts though the V-shaped ravines. Many are fast-moving freestone streams. Others become flat and slow-moving, like Silver Creek and the Henry's Fork in Idaho.

When fly-fishing was introduced into Japan from England, the anglers who accepted it rejoiced in this new tool for fishing from abroad. Others, finding it a less effective method of catching trout, continued to use live bait, which is still common today. In Japan, most anglers eat the trout that they catch. Because the trout that are caught are seldom released, the *yamame* and *iwana* have never seen an artificial fly and easily fall prey to the fly-fisher's imitation.

Traditional Japanese fly-fishers, called *tenkaras*, concentrate on the techniques of presenting an artificial to the trout rather than rely only on the effectiveness of a specific pattern. They are secretive about their methods, which will disappear when the inventor dies. As Japanese fly-fishers become more interested in using trout flies that imitate indigenous aquatic insects, original tyers whose flies mirror the Japanese sensibility will find greater acceptance in our country and will be recognized in the United States as well.

[Yokohama, Japan]

EPHEMERA SWIMMING NYMPH

HOOK *Tiemco 400T*

SIZE *#8 to #14*

THREAD *Tan 6/0*

WEIGHT *Lead wire, width and wrappings based on hook size*

TAIL *Natural ostrich tippets*

RIB *Round gold tinsel*

BODY AND THORAX *Dirty yellow dubbing fur*

WINGCASE *Dark brown goose quill or cinnamon yellow goose quill, depending on season*

GILL *Natural ostrich*

LEGS *Yellow partridge*

ISONYCHIA SWIMMING NYMPH

HOOK *Tiemco 400T*

SIZE *#8 to #14*

THREAD *Dark brown 6/0*

WEIGHT *Lead wire, width and wrappings based on hook size*

TAIL *Golden pheasant tippets*

RIB *Round gold tinsel*

BODY *Dark reddish brown dubbing fur*

OVERBODY AND THORAX *Dark brown turkey quill*

CENTERLINE *White polyester*

WINGCASE *Dark brown goose or turkey quill*

LEGS *Dark brown partridge*

EPHEMERELLA FLOATING NYMPH

HOOK *Tiemco 2487*

SIZE *#10 and #12*

THREAD *Olive 6/0*

TAIL *Pheasant tail, dyed olive*

BODY *Fly-Rite #34 Quill Gordon*

WINGCASE *White Styrofoam*

LEGS *Olive partridge*

R. Monty Montplaisir

If I had to use one word to describe my approach to flytying it would be *experimental.* Such experiments include designing new fly patterns and making improvements to some standard ties. Examples of the latter are my Chicken Feed Flies. Taking traditional fly patterns, I tie them with plastic strips taken from a feed bag. The resulting flies resemble their original counterparts but are not as fragile when fished.

Many of my fly designs have come from merging parts of several successful patterns into an entirely new pattern. Others, such as the Hare-Pala and Montberg, combine old and new materials to better simulate insects and baitfish. Also of interest to me are experiments in modifying conventional flytying techniques and originating new ones.

Improvising new methods was especially important to me years ago when the two major sellers of flies purchased most of their fly inventories from American tyers. Their combined yearly orders placed with me averaged between twenty-four and thirty-six thousand flies. Completion of such a volume required time and specialized tying techniques. Combining both with the personal pride I invested in each fly resulted in a product of quality. Today most flies are mass-produced by tyers in overseas factories operated by American importers. Most of their inventory is sold in the United States, and the money spent here for such imports now exceeds that spent for flies tied by Americans, which has adversely affected many tyers, including myself.

If asked to speculate about the future, I would predict that fly-fishing as a sport will continue to grow, as will the demand for flies. Flies will be supplied increasingly by importers and hobbyists, whose combined production has already resulted in many professional American tyers being forced out of the business. Flytying as an art form will continue to survive as long as it is practiced by a small number of dedicated people who are addicted to the activity and view it as a magnificent obsession.

[Averill, Vermont, U.S.A.]

OLIVE/SILVER HARE-PALA

HOOK *Mustad 9674*
SIZE *#2 to #8*
THREAD *White*
UNDERBODY *Lead wire*
OVERBODY *White chenille*
SIDES *Silver glitter tape*
WING *Rabbit fur strip, dyed olive*
GILLS *Red thread or dyed dubbing*
EYES *White and black doll eyes*

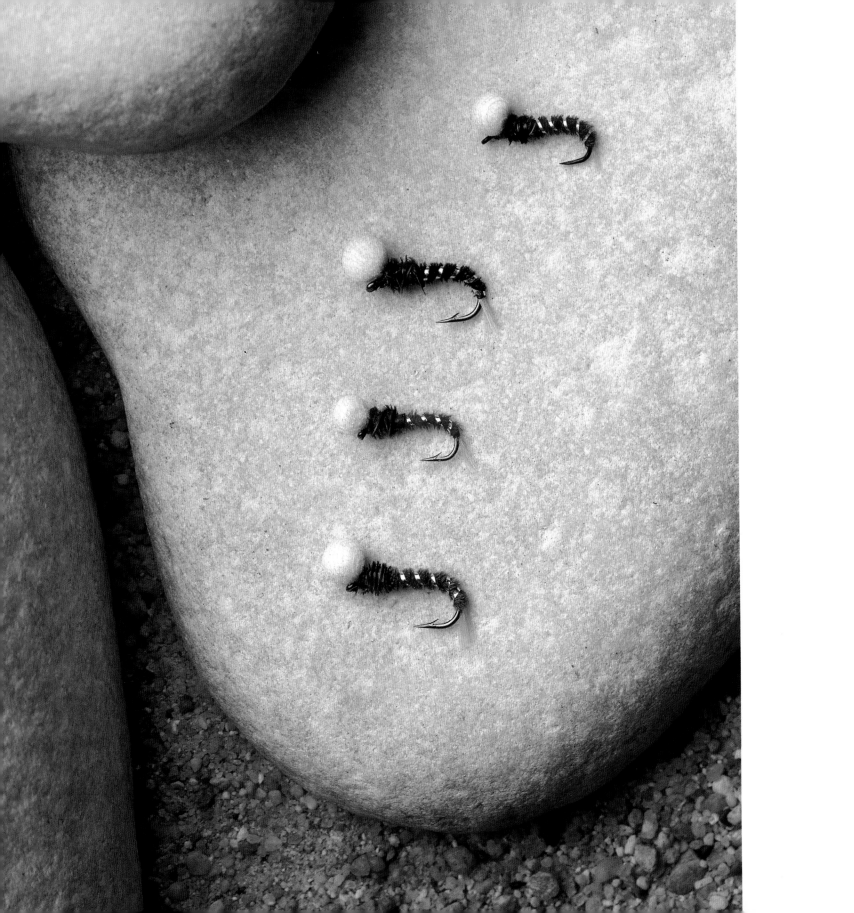

John Goddard

**SUSPENDER
HATCHING
MIDGE**

HOOK *Turned-down
eye, wide-gap hook*

SIZE *#12 to #18*

THREAD *Fine midge*

TAG *Strands of white
nylon filaments*

BODY *Black, brown,
red or green
marabou or
seal's fur*

RIB *Narrow silver
Lurex*

THORAX *Brown dyed
turkey herl*

HEAD *Ball of white
Ethafoam enclosed
in nylon mesh*

While I participate fairly regularly in still-water fly-fishing on England's many lakes and reservoirs, my first love remains the more leisurely pursuit of trout in rivers, particularly on the chalk streams of southern England. Although these streams may not have actually given birth to dry-fly fishing as we know it today, they most certainly have played a major role. Many giants of the fly-fishing world have trod these hallowed streams over the past century, and consequently many fly patterns that now enjoy a worldwide reputation were perfected on these same streams.

It is therefore hardly surprising that many of my early excursions into the fly-dressing world were undoubtedly influenced by my close association with these waters. I still prefer some of the traditional materials such as seal's fur and peacock herl. Now, over thirty years since I first started tying my own flies, I still use a lot of the old materials, but I must admit that some of the synthetics that have come onto the market in the last ten years or so have revolutionized the art. Many of these new synthetics are excellent, and many of my more recent patterns rely heavily on some of them.

My earlier patterns tended to represent natural insects as closely as possible. I gradually became convinced that other factors, such as overemphasizing key aspects of shape and color, were far more important than close imitation. I also became convinced that floatability in dry-fly patterns was a very important factor. Hence the development of the Goddard Caddis, which is popular on the large, brawling rivers of the western United States.

The pattern here represents the midge or chironomid pupa hanging in the surface film prior to hatching. These insects are one of the major food sources for fish in many of the large lakes and reservoirs in England. The Suspender Hatching Midge has been an astonishing success tied on #12 and #14 hooks. Only recently did I discover that this same pattern dressed on #16 and #18 hooks is unbelievably effective when fished on rivers to those infuriating trout that often rise all day just in or below the surface film to apparently invisible flies and ignore every artificial in your box.

[Cobham, Surrey, England]

Hal Janssen

I have spent the majority of my life pursuing fish—not just trying to catch them but trying to understand their behavior. When I fish an area, I constantly observe the insects and the fish, and their interrelationship. For many years, I collected various life forms of insects and transferred them to aquariums where I studied the nature and timing of their activity. As a result of these observations, I tie flies that not only imitate what the fish are feeding on, but in the water create a certain movement to which fish will respond. Although flytying is an art form, and I have tied flies that I regard as works of art, I also want to tie flies that are both fairly easy to make and durable.

While many flytyers limit themselves to materials and concepts that were used one hundred years ago, I tie many patterns that deviate from the norm. I look for different ways to tie a more effective fly, and I choose materials according to what I know they are capable of doing. Many of my patterns will become popular in ten to fifteen years, because it takes that long for fly-fishers to embrace new fly designs.

The sculpin, for example, is traditionally tied with deer hair. In making the Marabou Sculpin, which I developed to fish for rainbows in Alaska, I questioned whether deer hair was the simplest or best material to use for the pattern. As an alternative material, marabou has a tremendous breathing quality in the water, which results in that sense of life and movement I want in a fly. It is also possible to create shape with marabou, a feature many flytyers overlook.

Every fisherman has had, at some time in his life, a fly that he knows will be successful in a given area. I like that sense of anticipation so much—knowing any second a fish is going to take a fly—that I have strived for fifteen years or more to make that feeling precede every cast I make.

[Santa Rosa, California, U.S.A.]

MARABOU SCULPIN

HOOK *Partridge CH1A*
SIZE *#1 to #8*
THREAD *Olive*
BODY *Olive-gray, buff, natural gray, dark brown-olive and golden olive marabou, over ten or eleven wraps of 1-amp wire*
PECTORAL FINS *Hen feather from saddle*

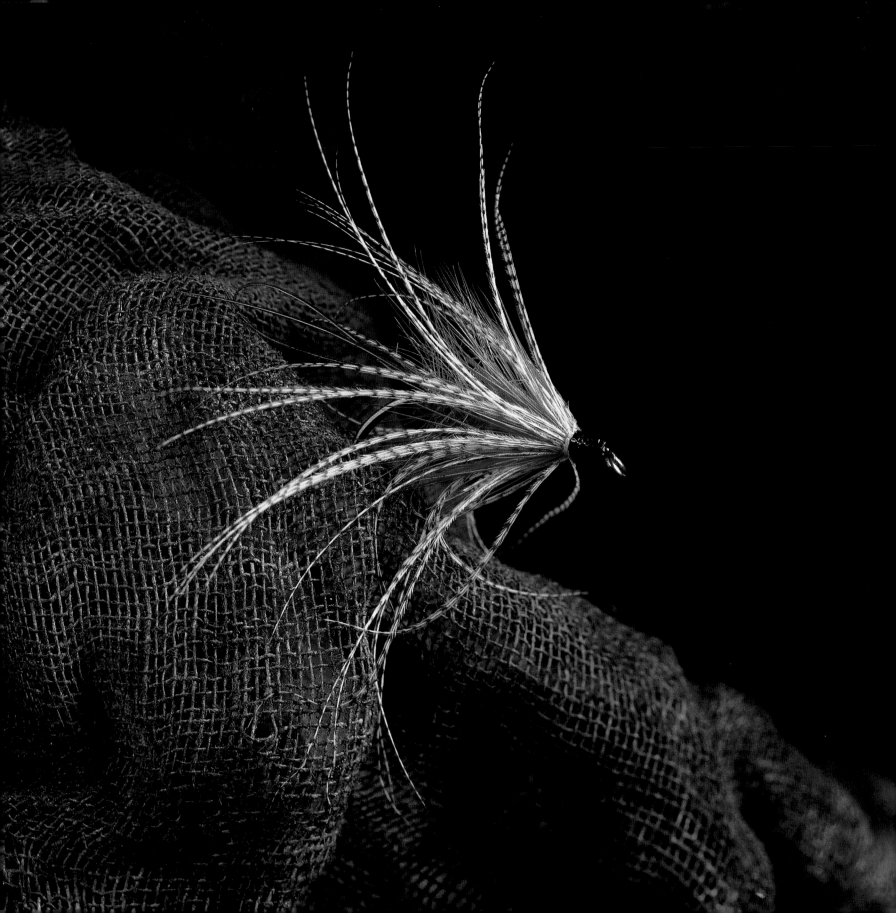

Robert McHaffie

GOSLING

HOOK *Partridge G3A*

SIZE *#4*

THREAD *Black*

TAIL *Three cock pheasant center tail fibers*

RIB *Fine gold wire*

BODY *Orange and yellow seal's fur, well mixed, and red game hackle dyed yellow*

HACKLE *Bright orange cock underneath gray mallard dyed yellow*

I began dressing flies when I was twelve years old because I wanted to catch fish on flies that I had created myself. As I grew up and yarned with older anglers, I gleaned bits of wisdom from them, by listening to them and watching little things that they did. For example, one old man, before commencing to fish for salmon with a new fly, would pull the jungle cock off it, saying, "That damn stuff only scares fish." So much for the value of this much-prized bird. He would then chew at the dressing with his front teeth, and he maintained that the fly would still not be good until it was pulled through a few bushes.

As I began to realize the value of a well-worn fly, I developed a method of tying over the years to create this style of fly. What I call this style can be summed up as "rough-dressed flies for fish's eyes." To achieve this effect, I use a lot of seal's fur and tinsel ribs to create a gauzy, translucent image, combined with overdyed hackles, such as Rhode Island red game overdyed olive or yellow. The bodies —formed in some cases with mixed colors instead of one solid color—are scrubbed with a piece of Velcro glued to an old lollipop stick. Flies tied in this manner pulsate and breathe in the water and glow at the same time with both transmitted and reflected hues.

Although I have been tying flies for over twenty-five years and am completely self-taught, I am still learning. Nothing gives me more pleasure than trying out a new material or fly pattern in order to find out if my ideas are similar to the trouts'. Perhaps if I keep at it long enough, I will turn into a fish.

[Limavady, Northern Ireland]

E. H. "Polly" Rosborough

Why did I start tying my own flies? Two reasons. There were no durable flies on the market, and too few effectively imitated or even simulated the insects in my local area.

My primary interest when I tied my first fly in the spring of 1928 was to create a fly that would last long enough to take at least a dozen or more fish. That intent is still my guideline. To this purpose, waterproof cement and at least five half-hitches go into the tying and finishing of every fly. I never tie flies smaller than #14. Nor do I tie flies that are exact imitations of insects. These often require plastics, raffia and other materials that, in the water, seem to die. Fish want their food to appear alive and healthy.

To this end, almost all of my tying is with fuzzy materials: spun fur and various fuzzy synthetic yarns, Mohlon, Orlon, acrylics. Following this thinking, I originated the twenty-five fuzzy nymphs shown in my book, *Tying and Fishing the Fuzzy Nymphs*, which first came out in 1965.

My favorite flies? I fish the hatches—nymphs, pupae, duns and adults—and these hatches come and go. So if I had to choose something I felt would always catch fish, it would not be a simulation of a specific insect. Rather, it would look more like a nice gob of food with the hazy outline of several insects in various forms. If allowed only one pattern of any nymph, wet, dry or streamer, it would be the #8 Fledermouse. It will consistently provoke strikes anytime, anywhere. Other patterns will outfish it during specific emergences, it is true, but I have known nothing else in my experience that will always catch fish.

My one bit of philosophy to all other tyers: Never feel that you have tied a fly that is good enough. You never will. Always try to tie the next one better.

[Chiloquin, Oregon, U.S.A.]

Fledermouse, Black and Bronze Wooly Worm and Casual Dress (clockwise from top left).

CASUAL DRESS

HOOK *Wright & McGill or Mustad*
SIZE *#2 to #12, 3x-long*
THREAD *Black Nymo*
TAIL, BODY AND SKIRT *Muskrat back fur, felted in hot soapsuds, rinsed and spun on hook*
HEAD *Three to five strands of black ostrich, twisted*

FLEDERMOUSE

HOOK *Wright & McGill or Mustad*
SIZE *#2 to #14, 3x-long*
THREAD *Tan Nymo*
BODY *Mixed dun fur, preferably Australian opossum, or a mix of muskrat belly and pale mink*
COLLAR *Australian opossum*
UNDERWING *Pearl mallard side*
OVERWING *Brown wigeon side*
HEAD *Tan thread*

BLACK AND BRONZE WOOLY WORM

HOOK *Wright & McGill*
SIZE *#2 to #12, 4x-long to x-short*
THREAD *Black Nymo*
TAIL *Marabou*
RIB *18-gauge copper tinsel or 30-gauge copper wire*
BODY *Strands of bronze peacock with black hackle wound palmer style between wraps of copper*
HEAD *Black thread*

EASTERN GOLDEN STONEFLY NYMPH

HOOK *Viellard Migeon*

SIZE *#8 6x-long for larger nymph, #12 6x-long for smaller nymph*

THREAD *Gold silk*

TAILS *Ringneck pheasant neck feathers, stripped*

ABDOMEN *Dyed golden angora with an overbody of handpainted cotton sheeting sprayed with fixative*

THORAX *Dyed golden angora*

LEGS, WINGCASE AND HEAD *Handpainted cotton sheeting, sprayed with fixative*

GILLS *Angora fur picked out from between legs*

ANTENNAE *Ringneck pheasant neck feathers, stripped*

Paul Schmookler

Just as I was never meant to be a part of the mainstream work force, I also was never to be a mainstream flytyer. From the very first fly I tied, I discovered that I could best express myself creatively through my tying. I did not read any books on flytying in my early days. I was so accustomed to doing things my own way that it did not matter if books would have made tying easier.

From my point of view, experimentation was all-important and I was determined to learn flytying on my own. Because of this, I started tying flies that matched my imagination. The more complex I imagined a pattern to be, the more enjoyment I received out of trying to tie it. Through this approach, I fell in love with creating beautiful jewels that came from my own imagination and had not previously been tied by someone else.

In the late 1970s, realistic imitations were being popularized by many of the prominent tyers. This resulted in factions among flytyers: there were those who tied classic patterns, those who followed a tying style that could at best be described as impressionistic, and those who pursued only realistic imitations. This latter group received much criticism from fellow anglers, particularly with such statements as "realistic imitations do not catch fish."

It was from such challenging remarks that I set out to create a series of imitations that were extremely lifelike and just as effective as other flies on the trout stream. This endeavor was realized when I finally completed artificials such as these two Eastern Golden Stonefly Nymphs *(Phasganophora capitata)* in different stages of development.

[Millis, Massachusetts, U.S.A.]

Richard W. Talleur

Basketball has its Doctor J., baseball its Doctor K., and fly-fishing its Doctor S.—the fabled Silver Doctor. This breathtakingly beautiful fly has survived a cross-oceanic transplant and wholesale depletion of the two species of salmonids it was designed to lure. Yet it is with us still, as a treasured object of angling art, if not a viable and productive fly pattern.

The Silver Doctor here differs somewhat from the original full-dress version, which was one of the superpatterns developed during the heyday of salmon fishing in the British Isles. That pattern was and is one of a select group of highly complex and challenging flies, many of which were as much a showcase for the tyer's mastery and ingenuity as they were practical angling weapons. In those wistfully remembered times, noble British sports would often present their favorite ghillies with bags of rare and exotic plumage from the corners of the earth. The resultant competition produced a plethora of incredible creations—truly the stained-glass-window school of flytying.

Fly-fishing gained wide popularity in the United States during the nineteenth century, not only for the Atlantic salmon, which is also indigenous to the British Isles, but for

SILVER DOCTOR

HOOK *Limerick or sproat-bend wet fly*
SIZE *#4 to #12*
THREAD *Red 6/0*
TIP *Fine gold tinsel*
TAIL *Small golden pheasant crest topped with blue kingfisher*
BUTT *Red seal's fur substitute, such as Seal-ex*
BODY *Flat silver tinsel*
RIBBING *Fine oval silver tinsel*
THROAT *Bright blue hackle fronted by guinea fowl*
WING *Red, blue and yellow goose shoulder strips, teal, mottled turkey or similar feather (bottom to top), all married*
HEAD *Several coats of red lacquer*

the native American char, commonly known as brook trout, which is not. Gorgeous, guileless, plentiful and tasty, the brookie was an easy mark for even the pedestrian fly-fisher, and for a time, resort hotels and fishing camps thrived throughout the Northeast.

The Golden Age of American Fly-fishing was yet to come, and the techniques and fly patterns used on the gullible brookie were, in the main, of British origin—in style, at least, if not in actual pattern. A number of uniquely American dressings evolved, such as the Parmachene Belle and the Fontinalis. These are married-wing wet flies, far simpler than the classic British full-dress patterns, but still somewhat testing of the tyer's skill, and very pretty. The Fontinalis is designed to replicate the fin of the brook trout *(Salvelinus fontinalis)*, a diabolically clever ruse that stimulates the trout's aggressive tendencies, particularly in ponds and lakes, where overpopulation often causes fierce competition for food. Although not nearly as true a likeness, the Parmachene Belle is, I believe, based on a similar concept. Reputedly, it was deadly in the lake for which it was named and in similar habitats.

The Silver Doctor was one of a number of traditional British patterns brought over for salmon fishing and subsequently adapted for use on trout. This resulted in a reduced dressing, an accommodation of practicality. For one thing, this country did not have the rigid social stratification of Great Britain. Fishing was open to everyone, and sportsmen either tied their own flies or bought them.

There was no ghillie caste whose only enfranchisement was to please their patrons, and thus no group of elite tyers. Exotic materials were not as readily available, nor were they necessary to produce flies that appealed to the then ubiquitous brook trout. Much smaller flies were called for in trout fishing—hence, the reduced patterns. Salmon fishermen who insisted on full-dress flies usually imported them from England.

In Ray Bergman's classic, *Trout,* first published in 1938, we find a number of these reduced dressings, including the Silver Doctor. The pattern description tracks quite closely with the traditional except for one detail—there is no red in the wing, either in the illustration or in the description. Because the rest of the dressing seeks to retain the integrity of the original, I have humbly assumed this to be an oversight and have put the red back in.

I tie the Silver Doctor and other patterns of this type mainly for the aesthetic experience—I happen to find them most attractive. I am also in love with full-dress salmon flies, but am frustrated by the unavailability of certain essential materials for which, to my knowledge, there are no acceptable substitutes. So, the Bergman flies must satisfy the artistic facet of my tying personality.

Which is not to say these flies cannot be fished. I have enjoyed success with the Doctor and the Parmachene Belle, and particularly the Fontinalis, in remote waters where seldom-fished-for brook trout prevail.

[Clifton Park, New York, U.S.A.]

Dave Whitlock

When I became interested in fly-fishing, I was nine years old and living in Oklahoma, which is not fly-fishing country. Although I had read about the sport in magazines, and it fascinated me, it was not until I was sixteen years old that I saw another fly-fisher. Because the literature then was very traditional and pious, I actually felt very unworthy of fly-fishing. That feeling haunted me for years.

When I began to tie flies, I would not even show my flies to people, because I did not have blue dun hackle, jungle cock feathers or the other special materials I had read about. But it seemed that those scraggly knots of hair, feather and sewing thread were enormously successful at catching fish. What I later began to realize as an adult was that anyone could be a fly-fisher and that individuality is important in this sport.

As a result of my early experiences, I decided to channel my career toward breaking down some of those barriers. If I have worked hard on anything in this sport, it has been to make flytyers and fly-fishers realize that they can be innovative, whether they are trout fishing in the Catskills or panfishing in Alabama. I try to make people feel at ease about what they are doing, through my tying, casting, writing and teaching, and to share knowledge rather than merely display it.

I have also tried to make people aware of the artistic and poetic aspects of flytying by designing attractive and eye-pleasing flies that really catch fish. Beautiful flies probably will not catch any more fish than flies that are one-tenth as artistic, but they are more enjoyable to tie and to fish. I design flies to catch fish and to please people, in that order. My business card reads, "the arts of fly-fishing." Photography and writing, flytying and rod building—all of these activities are art forms. Sometimes I innovate a fly on the spot, when I see an insect that fish are feeding on. Sometimes years of thought go into a fly. I engineer the fly in my mind, look for available materials that will work best, then

Red Fox Squirrel Hair
Nymph (left) and
Whitlock Matuka
Sculpin (right).

begin tying and testing until the fly looks
right to me—and to the fish.

As a flytyer, I am a nonconformist. Any
material can be used to tie a fly. Being a
flytyer is like being an artist who employs
many different media. I would make a fly out
of cedar if I could carve it to cast right and
look like what I wanted to imitate. Rather
than think of established materials, I consider
what a fly needs to perform properly. Although
with experience and age I have become more
of a perfectionist, for the most part I am
still very practical because I fish the flies I
make. For me, flytying is a very practical
form of work.

Flytyers are sculptors of the highest form.
There is, however, a difference between fly
sculptors and fly makers. I am a fly maker.
When tying flies for people, I want them to
fish with those flies. When I rate a fly, it
should be not only a fly that will enable me
to catch fish, but a fly that others can use to
catch fish too.

[Freeport, Maine, U.S.A.]

RED FOX SQUIRREL HAIR NYMPH

HOOK *Turned-down eye, 2x-long or 3x-long*
SIZE *#2 to #18*
THREAD *Black 6/0 nylon*
WEIGHT *Eight to ten turns of lead wire*
CEMENT *Dave's Flexament*
TAIL *Red fox squirrel back hair and underfur*
RIB *Fine or extrafine oval gold tinsel*
ABDOMEN *Equal mix of red fox squirrel belly hair and similar color Antron or Orlon dubbing*
THORAX *Red fox squirrel back hair*
HEAD *Black thread*

WHITLOCK MATUKA SCULPIN

HOOK *Long-shank, low-water Atlantic salmon or turned-down eye, 4x-long streamer*
SIZE *#5/0 to #8*
THREAD *Ivory Danville Plus*
WEIGHT *Lead wire*
CEMENT *Dave's Flexament*
MATUKA RIB *Medium gold wire*
BELLY *Pale yellow or creamy ivory dubbing*
BACK AND TAIL *Four pairs cree variant Chinese cock neck hackle*
PECTORAL FINS *Prairie chicken breast feathers or cock pheasant back feathers*
GILLS *Red Antron dubbing*
HEAD *Pale yellow or creamy ivory elk or deer hair for bottom, natural dun gray, dark brown and burnt orange or brandy deer hair for sides and top*

Cutthroat (top) and
rainbow (bottom).

MAGIC MINNOW

HOOK *Mustad #37187*

SIZE *#10*

THREAD *White 3/0
monocord for
tailing, white size A
rod-winding thread
for deer hair*

TAILING *Marabou
shorts or blood
feathers, dyed dark
olive grizzly, gray
and white for
rainbow, dyed light
olive grizzly, gray
and white for
cutthroat*

BODY *Elk or deer hair,
dyed chartreuse
and bleached white
for rainbow, dyed
yellow and
bleached white for
cutthroat*

COLOR *Pantone, AD
and Flair marking
pens, technical pen
and ink*

PECTORAL FINS *Pearl
Flashabou*

EYES *7-mm clear
plastic craft eyes*

WIGGLE LOOP *17-lb-test
Trilene XT
monofilament*

WIGGLE BILL *.010 mylar
sheeting*

Tim England

I enjoy flytying—every aspect of it. From selection and application of materials to execution of technique, the craft provides endless opportunities for creative expression. Beauty, enhanced by minute detail, can be found everywhere in this pastime, whether in an intricate pattern on a bird feather or in the rich ivory hue of bleached deer hair. While some of this beauty is obvious, even to a nonpractitioner, much of it is less conspicuous, like the gentle curve of elk hock fibers splayed out on the tail of a #18 Humpy.

The Magic Minnow derives its name not from its built-in swimming motion but from the visual subtleties provided by the materials. Constructed of deer hair, marabou and plastic, it pales in comparison with Mother Nature's original. Add imagination and it becomes more lifelike. If you could wet it down, you would see each hair become a tiny scale guarding its portion of pigment. The surface looks so smooth that it seems to glisten with life. The mylar bill is small, sturdy and ghostly. The eyes seem to stare, their iridescence adding to the deception. The gray parr marks complement the splashes of color that identify this mock minnow as a baby trout.

Fishing the Magic Minnow requires even more imagination. It is designed to be fished slowly and deliberately. You guide and direct it remotely, through the line in your hand. The objective is to make the Minnow imitate life. As you cause it to swim, try to sense the quietness, feel the denseness, and see the opaqueness of its environs. Move it along as though it were searching for midges at the surface. Stop it. The marabou caudal wavers, the eyes stare soberly—it has become the perfect fraud. The Flashabou moves almost undetected, pulsated by some invisible current. Can you see it?

An explosion of water spray and droplets in the air jolt you back to reality. A smile creeps across your face as a surge of living energy flows through your rod and the line speeds from your hand. To me, flytying is all of this and more.

[Bellvue, Colorado, U.S.A.]

Randall Kaufmann

Twenty years ago, very few anglers included nymph imitations in their fly boxes, and the few who did probably had only a vague idea of the life cycle of actual nymphs and their relation to fish as a source of food. Today nymphs are at the forefront of anglers' attention.

Generally, the slower and clearer the water, the more difficult it is to deceive fish into accepting your imitation. The faster and less clear the water, the easier it is to fool fish. Regardless of conditions, the longer a fly is presented to the fish, the less likely it is that the fish will take the fly. From what little we know about the perceptions of the trout, it would seem logical that nymph recognition consists of the following "keys": size, shape, color, animation and presentation. The more "keys" you have, the higher your rate of success.

It is with *all* these thoughts in mind that I devise or select an imitation to fish. The Kaufmann Stone illustrates this strategy nicely. The size of the fly follows that of the natural, and the shape of the nymphs is consistent. The preferred color is achieved through a blend of several colors, thereby allowing fish perhaps to see either a natural mottling effect or a specific color. The material is chosen for its reflective or translucent properties and for its underwater behavior or animation qualities. Movement of the water and your retrieve, or manipulation of the line, as you fish the fly complete the animation.

An understanding of how a particular nymph becomes available to trout as a food source provides insight into how the artificial should be presented. Much of this may sound intimidating to the uninitiated, but once you grasp the basic ideas, common sense and observation become your guiding factors. Then, the hypnotic effect of the sound and movement of water and the magical world of the trout will transport you to a mesmerized state of pleasure and satisfaction.

[Portland, Oregon, U.S.A.]

KAUFMANN STONE

HOOK *Tiemco 300, weighted and flattened*
SIZE *#2 to #10*
THREAD *To match body*
TAIL *Stripped goose to match body*
RIB *Swannundaze to match body*
BODY *Equal mixture of several colors (claret, amber, orange, rust, black, brown, blue, purple, ginger) of angora goat and predominant color of Hare-tron dubbing*
WINGCASE *Three sections of lacquered turkey*
THORAX AND HEAD *Same as body*
ANTENNAE *Same as tail*

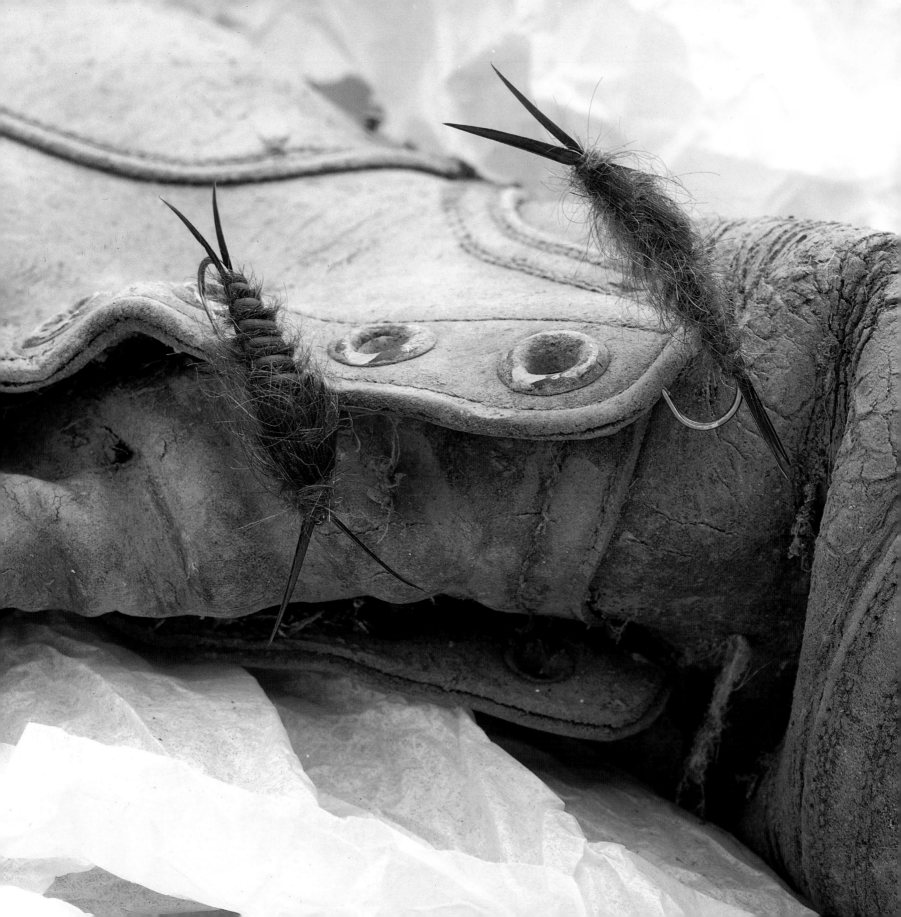

Poul Jorgensen

STONEFLY NYMPH

HOOK *3x-long*

SIZE *#2 and #4*

THREAD *Brown 6/0*

TAILS *Two moose mane fibers*

UNDERBODY *Thin plastic, trimmed to shape*

ABDOMEN *Latex tinted tan*

THORAX *Gray fur dubbing*

WINGCASES *Pheasant body feathers, set in cement and burnt to shape*

LEGS *Six goose biots dyed tan*

PRONOTUM AND HEAD *Pheasant body feathers, set in cement*

EYES *Nylon*

ANTENNAE *Two moose mane fibers*

It is hard to believe that nearly thirty-two years have passed since I met the late Bill Blades at a small lake north of Chicago, Illinois. It is even harder to believe that meeting this elderly, white-haired gentleman completely changed my life.

At first we talked pleasantly about the weather and the fishing. Neither of us mentioned anything about flies. Bill had finished fishing for the day. "Had enough," he said. Besides, it was too hot. I helped him carry his gear from the boat to the trunk of his Cadillac. The trunk was empty except for a spare tire and a tray with insects that was carefully placed on top of a bundle of blankets in the corner. When I asked about the insects, he said, "These are not real insects. They are artificials. See the hook there?"

I could hardly believe it. They looked so real. My eyes were glued to the stonefly nymphs lined up in a row like soldiers. My mind was already made up—I must learn how to make them—and over the next seven years, as a student of Bill Blades, I did just that.

Stonefly nymphs are some of the most beautiful insects we have in our streams and rivers, which is why so many fishable patterns have been devised over the years. The structural appearance of the insect, for all practical purposes, is almost identical throughout the many different species. Stonefly nymphs are generally flat and have a long segmented abdomen with two tails. They are best distinguished from other nymphs by their beautifully marked wingcases, located on top of the thorax portion, which makes up the front half of the nymph. The head of a stonefly is quite large and flat, with two antennae about as long as the tails. In addition to these unique features, there is an important factor that makes stonefly nymphs different from other nymphs, such as mayfly nymphs, and larvae: they have a smooth abdomen without hairy filaments. The breathing gills of the stonefly are located next to the robust legs.

My Stonefly Nymph is the result of twenty-five years of practice with different types of materials. There are lots of improvements still to come. As Bill Blades would say, "Flytying is a school from which we never graduate."

[Roscoe, New York, U.S.A.]

Gary Borger

Flytying embodies both practical artistry and scientific understanding. From an artistic point of view, flies should have a sense of balance about them and be proportioned like their natural counterparts. They should also stress the features that give the impression of life. Like works by pointillistic painters, flies are constructed of distinctly individual elements that blend to form a whole greater than the sum of the individual parts.

Artificials should be durable and constructed as simply as possible while retaining the necessary impressionistic features. Achieving this may involve the blending of natural materials with technologically advanced synthetics—a process requiring the tyer, like the artist, to have a broad knowledge of materials and how to apply them and to continually strengthen this understanding by searching for new materials and applications.

From the scientific standpoint, flies should emphasize those features that trigger the trout to feed. Such a design requires a comprehensive understanding of the life cycles and behavior of the fish's food organisms as well as an understanding of the feeding responses of the fish. It entails an unbiased approach to fly design, where success is not based on a single observation but on many trials over a period of years. Only by such careful observation can our understanding of the fish and its feeding responses be truly advanced.

To me, the art and science of designing flies is more than a methodology—it is also great fun.

[Wausau, Wisconsin, U.S.A.]

Marabou Damsel Nymph, Red Brown Nymph and Hair-Leg Hare's Ear (clockwise from top).

RED BROWN NYMPH

HOOK *Standard length shank*

SIZE *#6 to #20*

THREAD *Dark rusty brown 6/0*

TAIL *Four to six fibers from pheasant tail feather*

BODY *Fuzzy yarn or dubbing, dark rusty brown, weighted under thorax*

WINGCASE *Six to eight strands of peacock herl*

LEGS *Guard hairs from back of cottontail rabbit*

HAIR-LEG HARE'S EAR

HOOK *Standard length shank*

SIZE *#6 to #20*

THREAD *Dark rusty brown 6/0*

TAIL *Four to six fibers from pheasant tail feather*

RIB *Embossed gold tinsel*

BODY *Coarse dubbing blended from hare's mask, tan sparkle yarn and gray squirrel fur, weighted under thorax*

WINGCASE *Six to eight strands of peacock herl*

LEGS *Guard hairs from back of cottontail rabbit*

MARABOU DAMSEL NYMPH

HOOK *Standard length shank*

SIZE *#10 and #12*

THREAD *Olive 6/0*

TAIL *Mixture of pale olive-yellow and brown marabou, three or four fibers of each color*

BODY *Fuzzy yarn or dubbing, pale olive-yellow, weighted under thorax*

WINGCASE *Six to eight strands of peacock herl*

LEGS *Guard hairs from pale olive dyed rabbit skin*

George F. Grant

**FEATHERBACK
NYMPH**

HOOK *Mustad 3665A
or 9575*

SIZE *#6*

THREAD *Color to
match pattern*

TAILS *Two fibers of
appropriate size
and color*

BODY CORE *Yellow floss
wound around
itself to required
size and cylindrical
shape*

BODY SHAPE *Two ¾"
straight pins bound
on either side of
body core, heads
toward eye*

BACK AND BODY *Game
bird feather,
depending on
pattern used; glued
to foundation and
overwrapped with
clear flat 30-lb-test
monofilament*

HACKLE *Handwoven
from natural badger
guard hairs*

I became interested in flytying in about 1928, and it has been a consuming passion ever since. In retrospect, it is apparent that I was simply predestined to lead an idyllic life wading fabulous western trout streams; dressing artificial creations to copy the aquatic insects and deceive the large wild trout that lived within these waters; and enjoying the mystique and the endless variety that is part of the sport called fly-fishing, which, to many of us, is a passport to another world.

I have long held the opinion that flytying is closely related to both art and science. I think that a skilled flytyer who works creatively with hair and feather is just as surely an artist as the individual who works with watercolor and oils. I believe, too, that knowledge of the use of various materials in relation to their buoyancy, action and appearance in the element in which they are used leads the flytyer into a field that is not unlike that of a laboratory researcher.

My system of flytying is based to a great extent on a method of weaving hair into the form of a hackle devised by Franz B. Pott, a professional flytyer who lived most of his life in Missoula, Montana. My own contribution to the woven-hair concept has been the extension of the idea into a greater variety of uses; the utilization of synthetic flies; and the development of methods to weave short, soft hair, such as squirrel and deer, into short-fibered hackles.

The flies shown here are examples of pin-shaped stonefly nymph patterns with featherbacks protected and enhanced by an outer shell of clear oval monofilament. The hackles are woven from various animal hairs. I also apply the woven-hair method to a complete range of wet and dry flies, rough-hair nymphs, minnows and sculpins.

The beginner who regards flytying as a means of making flies cheaper than they can be bought is doomed to mediocrity. The only flytyers who achieve any lasting distinction are those who value creativity above all else. There must be a continuing pursuit of an idea, a system or a method.

[Butte, Montana, U.S.A.]

Alf Davy

When I tie and fish artificials to fool my worthy adversary, the trout, it is important to make a fly that can impart the right movement in the water as well as a fly that possesses the correct color and shape. I like to fish my nymph patterns near the bottom where the trout feed. Because insects and other sources of food for the trout move slowly through the water—as they, in turn, search for food—I want to retrieve the fly so that it represents the action of the natural as closely as possible. The problem with such a slow retrieve is that the fly catches or tangles on the weeds and other objects at the bottom of a lake.

After experimenting with many materials and methods that would allow a slow retrieve, I found that deer hair, as the most buoyant material, keeps the fly suspended in the water. A long, stiff beard added underneath the fly deflects the weeds from the hook point. As the imitation is slowly walked along the bottom—the action that gives the fly its name—the stiff fibers push the hook away from any obstruction that could impair its movement. Because the fish only views the natural from the top, it does not see the beard. When I fish this and other Bottom Walker patterns closer to the surface, I eliminate the beard, which would cause the fish to see an unnatural profile on the fly.

Having successfully used these same tying techniques not only for this and other dragonfly nymphs but also for leeches, scuds, caddisflies and mayflies, I know that during those hot days of summer, when the trout go deep, I will keep having fun with the fish.

[Kelowna, British Columbia, Canada]

BOTTOM WALKER

HOOK *Long shank*
SIZE *#6 to #10*
THREAD *Black 6/0*
BODY *Deer hair, spun on hook and clipped to shape, and olive or other color dubbing or colored felts*
LEGS *Pheasant tail*
BEARD *Moose mane*
HEAD *Deer hair, spun on hook and clipped, and dubbed over with color*

The Dry Fly

Al Troth

I consider myself a fly-fisherman first and a flytyer second. As an outfitter-guide, I spend over a thousand hours every year fly-fishing with clients and friends, and flies that consistently catch trout are a must if I am to be successful in this occupation. I spend seven months of the year tying full-time professionally. I guess you might say that almost every waking hour of my life revolves around fishing and trout flies.

Forty-five years at the tying vise, combined with countless hours on the water, reading every book attainable on trout fishing and flytying, and associating and exchanging information with some of the best anglers in the world, have provided experiences that have allowed me to glean the best concepts and techniques necessary for effective fly design. The more vast one's background, the easier this job becomes.

My needs have spawned a philosophy in flytying that requires a fly to be a proven catcher of trout, reasonably quick and simple to tie, durable, and constructed of materials that are readily available. My Elk Hair Caddis dry fly, which has received acclaim around the world, typifies the principles of design and construction that make up my approach to tying.

[Dillon, Montana, U.S.A.]

ELK HAIR CADDIS

HOOK *Partridge L2A Captain Hamilton*

SIZE *#8 to #18*

THREAD *Tan 3/0*

RIB *.005-inch-diameter brass wire*

BODY *Hare's ear dubbing*

WING *Bleached cow elk*

HACKLE *Brown or furnace*

Walking Spider (top) and Trout Hawk (bottom).

Helen Shaw

WALKING SPIDER

HOOK *Allcock*

SIZE *#10, slightly reversed, short shank, turned-up eye*

THREAD *Pearsall's Gossamer*

HACKLE *All brown, ginger or badger, or with a white front*

TROUT HAWK

HOOK *Allcock Model Perfect*

SIZE *#6 x-long to #10*

THREAD *3/0 nylon*

WINGS AND TAIL *Calf tail, natural or dyed*

BODY *Trimmed deer body hair, natural or dyed, depending on pattern*

The Walking Spider is patterned after those wonderful dry flies attributed to Edward R. Hewitt, whom I met at the Anglers' Club of New York, on Ladies' Night, years ago. It is sparsely tied, as closely as possible to his description of it, and when fished properly, it dances and skitters on the water—a pretty sight to see as it drifts down gently, and walks or skates across the surface. It is an extraordinary dry fly, and created quite a sensation when it first appeared.

An interesting challenge to a flytyer, both in the choice of hackle and in the precise manner of its application to the hook, the Walking Spider may be tied with all brown, all ginger, or badger hackles, or with a white front as a bivisible.

The little Hawks are unusual, deer hair–bodied, dry flies. Other trout flies have deer hair bodies, but as far as I know, none were ever trimmed as I do these, and the unique shape of the body contributes to their fine casting performance and retrieving quality. In larger sizes the Hawks are excellent for bass, but in this size and smaller, they are remarkably effective trout flies, used by knowledgeable fishermen at dusk.

Tied in several tested color combinations besides the one shown here, the durable little Hawks have proven to be almost indestructible and, for fishermen not averse to using an "unorthodox" dry fly for trout, surprisingly rewarding. The "old-timers" of the Midwest often found that flies originally designed for bass could be tied in smaller sizes and used very successfully for large browns on the trout streams of the midwestern states and the boundary waters between the United States and Canada.

[East Chatham, New York, U.S.A.]

Neil Patterson

In 1886, the year Frederic Halford's *Floating Flies and How to Dress Them* first fluttered off the presses, Gottlieb Daimler proudly pulled the wraps off the Daimler Motor Carriage, the first horse carriage to be powered by a gasoline engine. Between then and now, Daimler's nine mph dinosaur has been developed into something that moves faster than the speed of sound. What about Halford's water babies?

For the dry fly, it has been a century of tinkerings. The basic design and function remain virtually unchanged. Is this fair to say?

Perhaps this assessment is a little hard on the many fly dressers who have reviewed the fundamental design of the dry fly set out in Hampshire, England, so many decades ago. But most of these efforts have been unfairly pitched way beyond the grasp of the fly dresser who lacks high grades in fingertip physics, the flimsy, high-tech products often proving to be totally impractical for everyday riverside use.

This has certainly been the case when it comes to answering the dry fly's biggest design clangor of all—the fact that it lands the wrong way up, exposing the hook and, with it, the angler's intentions to the trout in the most graphic, three-dimensional way imaginable.

Here lie the roots of my attitude toward fly dressing—my attitude, not my style, for I do not have a single style of tying a fly. There can never be one simple, all-embracing answer to the task of making something out of fur or feather that a trout will consider worthy enough to take into its mouth to investigate further.

The Funneldun, my imitation of the up-wing fly *(Ephemeroptera)*, is my flytying philosophy wrapped around a hook. The Funneldun can never be called a "pattern." It is more fundamental than that.

It is a blueprint for tying dry flies based on a concept. Since I am comparing flytying with car design, I call the concept *Volks-fliegen,* "flies for the people." These are flies

FUNNELDUN

HOOK *Any type and size*

THREAD *Any color*

TAIL *Any cock hackle fiber*

BODY *Any natural or synthetic*

THORAX *Any dark, soft fur*

HACKLE *Any long-flued hackle, cock or hen*

designed to fit a particular belief, perform a particular job, pull off a particular stunt. Having promised this, they are capable of being dressed by any angler, novice or professional, and can be used on any particular day, after day, after day.

My fear is that the art of fly dressing, as a result of efforts to do new things, is rocketing out of the realm of simplicity, leaving the happy, practical-minded, average fly dresser like myself feeling hopelessly confused, finger-knotted and unfairly inadequate. Although I am on the side of progress in this sport, I do not think that using polar bear underbelly fur instead of wool picked off a barbed wire fence, or employing violently complex tying techniques to reach small ends, is the way to take fly dressing into the twenty-first century. If it is, it does not fool me.

This is where flytying becomes art for art's sake and has very little to do with why I tie flies: to catch trout. Creative flytyers should work toward simplicity, minimizing movements, expressing new concepts in the most down-to-earth flytying terms, and try to bring into the ranks more fly-fishers who do not dress flies rather than scare them off.

So what does the Funneldun promise?

It lands upside down, hook in the air with every chuck. It incorporates a thorax, an important feature in the natural's outline. The cheaper, the more readily available and the more substandard the cape you pick the hackle from, the better (cockfighting had been abolished forty years before *Floating Flies*, and even then Halford was depending on a rare commodity). It positions the hackle in a way that eliminates the dry fly's hereditary Titanic tendencies. You have to throw a brick at it to sink it. Finally, the Funneldun is just as easy to tie as any standard dry fly. And you will not find anyone taking it to the nearest consumer complaints department.

[Newbury, Berkshire, England]

André Puyans

Mother Nature is the supreme artist. Therefore, I look at the function she originally intended a material to perform in order to judge its suitability for my intended use. The basis of flytying is the selection and preparation of materials. A feather from a bird that is water-oriented, for example, is naturally waterproof and suitable for a dry fly. On the other hand, wool is inappropriate, because sheep would sink if they wound up in the water.

Principles in the selection and preparation of materials make up the focus of the classes I have been teaching for twenty-five years. Many of my teaching techniques originated in the early 1960s, when I taught hospitalized Vietnam War veterans how to tie flies. I had to make the subject interesting and clear for men who neither knew what a fly was nor were likely ever to leave that hospital. Picking the most challenging fly—the dry fly—I divided it into parts, from making quill wings to handling calf tail and spinning deer hair. Since then I have applied these same methods to teach thousands of students. My motivation to teach is an expression of gratitude to all those who took their time to educate me.

In my own tying, I like to take an idea and polish it to the best of my ability. I compress a pattern into the essential qualities to which a fish responds: size, shape, color and texture, in that order. In doing this, it is important to distinguish between a tying style and the various patterns within that style. One of the most important western dry flies, the Humpy, or Goofus Bug, is an offspring of the Horner Deer Hair, invented by Jack Horner. I have modified his original tying style. As a result, the fly is more durable, more effective, and has a broader range of uses, although the basic concept should be credited to Horner. The Blue Dun Humpy is one pattern within this modified tying style.

Simple solutions to designing a fly are often the best. The Loop Wing series is so simple that I could not believe that I was the

BLUE DUN HUMPY

HOOK *Tiemco 5210*

SIZE *#12 pictured, suggested range #10 to #20*

THREAD *Olive 3/0*

TAIL *Dark natural deer hair*

BODY *Dark natural deer hair over olive tying thread*

WINGS *Dark natural deer hair*

HACKLE *Medium rusty blue dun*

LOOP WING MACAW ADAMS

HOOK *Tiemco 5210*

SIZE *#12 pictured, suggested range #10 to #20*

THREAD *Gray 6/0*

TAIL *Brown and grizzly hackle fibers or perfectly marked cree hackle*

BODY *One or two center fibers from blue-yellow macaw tail, depending on size of fly*

WINGS *Six fibers of teal flank, divided three per side*

HACKLE *Brown and grizzly mixed, or perfectly marked cree*

originator. The Loop Wing Macaw Adams applies a new tying style to an old pattern. It was inspired when I fished the Owens River in California with the late Jim Quick. Fishing along a section of undercut bank that looked like a trout haven, I caught only two fish. Jim handed me an Adams with a macaw body, which he called his "problem solver." It produced then and has been so successful since that I adapted it as a pattern in the Loop Wing series.

I seek to tie the perfect fly, even though the perfect fly has never been tied. I refuse to let a fly out until I am unable to improve it in any way. I do not want to cast that fly five times and have it perform well only three. When I create a fly, I want it to fish right with every cast.

[Walnut Creek, California, U.S.A.]

Loop Wing Macaw Adams (left) and Blue Dun Humpy (right).

Roman Moser

My home river in Austria, the Traun, comes out of Traun Lake as a big river, like the Yellowstone. The fish found here are browns, rainbows, graylings and lake-running browns that grow to a respectable size. All of the insects important to these fish inhabit the river, but the caddisfly plays the dominant role in providing food for the trout.

My Balloon Caddis, with its shiny, oversized thorax, represents the caddisfly as it leaves its pupal shuck and begins to spread its wings. In nature the caddis moves and shivers as it floats downstream. The fish take the buoyant imitation with a splashy rise. In the evening, when just-hatched caddisflies swim across the water heading for the bank or looking for a place to lay eggs, I gently pull the fly against the current to create a noticeable wake that attracts the fish. Because the fish are looking for a black silhouette, I use a dark version of the fly.

Sparsely dressed in smaller sizes and in a cream color, this pattern imitates a hatching mayfly. Emerging mayflies, midges and caddisflies look the same to the fish, their wings just opening and their thoraxes appearing as large, shiny balls. I have fished the Balloon Caddis successfully on the Madison and Yellowstone rivers as well as the Traun. Using this same balloon technique, I make ants, beetles, hoppers and stoneflies.

The fish help me to decide what materials or style of dressing to use. I study both the behavior of insects and how they are seen by the fish. It has always been important for me to experiment with different prototypes of an insect at one of its life stages, such as the emerging caddis. At first I made realistic imitations that looked good to the fly-fisher but were often refused by the fish. My research showed me that fish prefer impressionistic patterns that emphasize the predominant aspects of an insect and its behavior. In designing flies and fishing them, one must put aside human ways of perceiving and try to see through the eyes of the fish.

[Gmunden, Austria]

BALLOON CADDIS

HOOK *Partridge Roman Moser Arrow Point barbless*

SIZE *#12*

THREAD *Yellow*

ABDOMEN *Olive synthetic dubbing*

WINGS *Deer hair, natural or dyed (optional)*

THORAX AND HEAD *Golden yellow Polycelon foam*

Lee Wulff

ROYAL WULFF

HOOK *Turned-up eye or turned-down eye*

SIZE *#8 to #16*

THREAD *Black*

TAIL *Light brown bucktail or elk*

BODY *Peacock herl and red floss*

WING *White bucktail*

HACKLE *Dark brown saddle hackle*

What makes a fish take a fly? It takes a fly because the fly looks like something to eat or something to chase and catch just for fun. And a fly looks like this if it combines the correct elements of size, motion (imparted by the angler or by the fly itself), and insectlike appearance. In making flies, the things in my mind are both the general appearance and the way the fly will work as I fish it.

I created the Wulff series of flies during the winter of 1929 and 1930, in rebellion against the typical British-type dry flies. Looking at the dry flies of the time with what I hoped was a trout's perspective, I thought they looked skimpy. In addition, they were difficult to keep afloat and seemed hardly worthwhile for a big trout to make a long rise to the surface for.

I wanted a buggier-looking, heavier-bodied fly, with better flotation. Looking for a material that would float such a body, I came up with bucktail. Out of this thinking evolved the Royal Wulff, Gray Wulff and White Wulff, and later the Grizzly Wulff, Black Wulff, Brown Wulff, Blonde Wulff and others.

The Royal Wulff made the old, difficult-to-float, but beautiful Royal Coachman pattern into an enormously effective fly. As an attractor, it has become one of the most used and most successful flies in America. It may come as a complete surprise to the trout, but it has this advantage: its chocolate brown, pure white, scarlet red, and dark iridescent green make a pattern that can be seen readily in any light against any background by both fish and angler.

Over my many years of fishing, I have learned that angling's problems are never solved. They rise anew with each new pool and each new day. Fishing, especially fly-fishing, has problems and solutions, challenges and rewards, which have always captured my imagination and stimulated my creativity.

[Lew Beach, New York, U.S.A.]

Walt and Winnie Dette, Mary Dette

Back in the 1920s, when Winnie and I started making flies, flytying seemed somewhat secretive, and few books were available where we could find information about techniques. I went to Rube Cross, one of the most important Catskill tyers at the time, and offered to pay him to teach me. He refused, so I bought flies from him and other tyers, took them apart and figured out how and with what they were made.

Winnie lived with her family at Riverview Inn, on the Beaverkill River about a mile below Roscoe, New York. The fishermen who were guests there became very interested that she was learning how to tie flies and encouraged her. She sold some flies from the hotel office, but it was not until after we were married, in the fall of 1928, that we set

DELAWARE ADAMS

Tied by Walt Dette

HOOK *Mustad 94840*
SIZE *#10 to #16*
THREAD *White 7/0 silk*
TAIL *Gray grizzly hackle*
BODY *Green wool dubbing, palmered with gray grizzly hackle*
WING *Gray grizzly hackle*
HACKLE *Gray grizzly and brown*

LIGHT HENDRICKSON

Tied by Winnie Dette

HOOK *Mustad 94840*
SIZE *#10 to #20*
THREAD *White 7/0 silk*
TAIL *Natural light dun*
BODY *Dubbed red fox fur from belly*
WINGS *Lemon wood duck*
HACKLE *Natural light dun*

COFFIN FLY

Tied by Mary Dette

HOOK *Mustad 79580*
SIZE *#12 and #14*
THREAD *White 6/0 silk*
TAIL *Peccary*
BODY *White Phentex with clipped white hackle*
WINGS *Dark teal*
HACKLE *Badger*

up a flytying room at the hotel. It became quite a gathering place for hotel guests, and in the spring of 1929 we began to sell flies as a sideline to our regular jobs. During the Depression we turned to flytying to make our living. I was able to obtain so many wholesale orders from businesses in New York City that we invited Harry Darbee, who then lived in New Paltz, to join us as a third partner.

When I went to my first sports show, I think I was the only tyer there. Quite a group stood in front of where I was tying. I had laid out my materials—a major preliminary step—and was tying the Fan-Wing Royal Coachman when a man stepped out from the audience with a stopwatch. He said, "You know, I've just timed you. You tied that fly in two and one-half minutes. You have nerve charging twenty-five cents for it." That was a long time ago. He should see how flytying has changed since.

Although I was not alive during the years that Theodore Gordon popularized fly-fishing in the Catskills, Winnie and I and our daughter Mary are part of that tradition, which also includes such tyers as Cross and Roy Steenrod. We are known for tying many of the classic Catskill patterns. Our way of tying is very practical. The flies are simple but have qualities that make them effective. The Delaware Adams, an offshoot of the original Adams, has become very popular because it has excellent floating qualities. In all of the work we do, we always make sure that our flies of a certain pattern are exactly like one another.

I have invented such flies as the Coffin and Delaware Adams. But we try to stay away from originating patterns, because I feel the market is flooded with new flies and many of them are very similar. You can invent a new pattern every day or week, but it will not necessarily be better at catching fish. I have tried to talk to the fish over many years about what they think, but have not gotten an answer yet. One person will say a certain fly is the greatest, the next will say it is the poorest. You could live on a stream and find out something new all the time. There is a lot to learn.

—*Walt Dette*
[Roscoe, New York, U.S.A.]

Chauncy K. Lively

Flytying has its basis in nature, and we who practice the craft are fortunate to have the availability of living prototypes to serve as models for fly design. Observing a mayfly dun at short range tells us what we need to know about the insect's size, shape, color and posture on the water. There are other considerations, too, which only become apparent when the insects are studied from the trout's perspective.

I built my first glass slant-tank about twenty-seven years ago and it has become one of my most valuable tools. The trout's cone of vision and its window to the outside world are physical phenomena attributed to the refraction of light entering the water. These matters have been explored in depth by such angling authorities as E. W. Harding, Edward R. Hewitt, Vincent C. Marinaro and coauthors John Goddard and Brian Clarke. However vividly these phenomena are described in print and illustrated by line draw-

ings, the actual imagery provided by observing floating insects and artificial flies from underneath the slant-tank is far more meaningful.

By shifting the angle of observation, we can simulate a trout's view of the insect progressively floating into the window. The parts of the insect touching the surface create slight indentations which are visible to trout as impressions on the mirrorlike underside of the film long before the floating insect enters the trout's window. The arrangement of indentations is known as the "light pattern," and each type of insect has its own distinctive light pattern. Thus, the light pattern of mayfly duns may differ drastically from that of spent mayfly spinners, just as flush-floating terrestrials give different impressions than caddisflies or stoneflies. Since it is the light pattern that triggers the beginning of the rise, it is as important to accurately represent this aspect as it is to simulate the insect's color and form.

The March Brown and Sulphur Dun

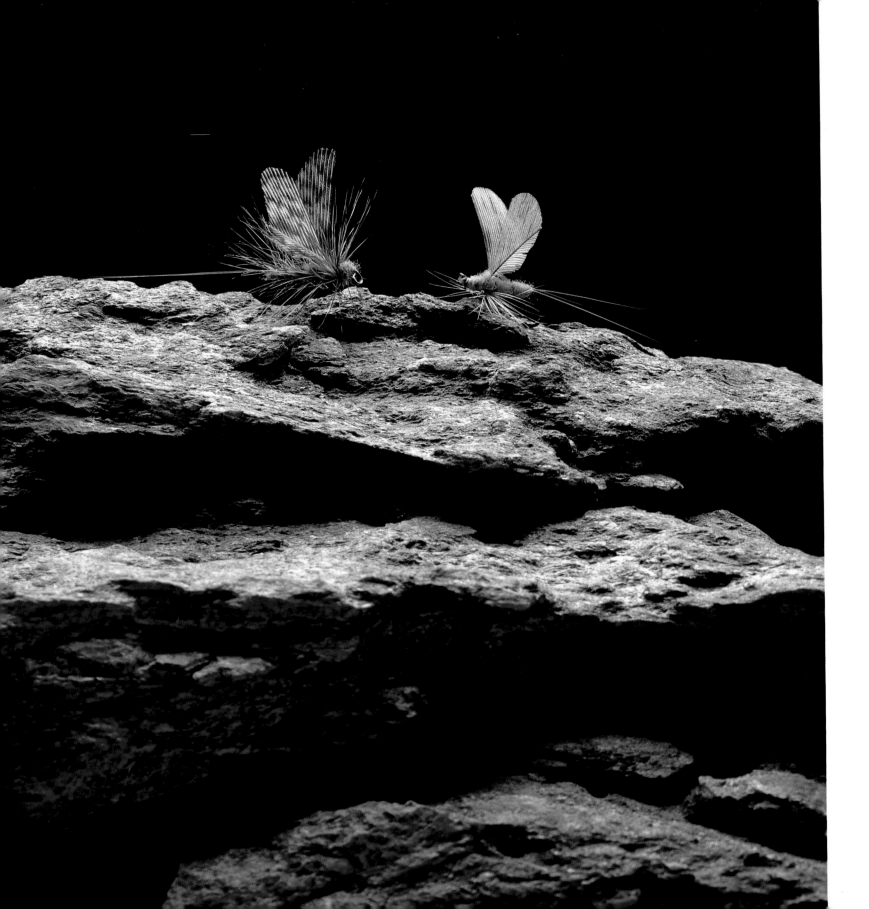

MARCH BROWN

HOOK *Regular shank, fine wire*

SIZE *#10 and #12*

THREAD *Tan 6/0*

TAILS *Pale microfibbets, widely split*

DUBBING *Tan fur or synthetic*

WINGS *Pheasant back feathers, cut or burnt to shape*

HACKLE *Brown and grizzly, one each*

SULPHUR DUN

HOOK *Regular shank, fine wire*

SIZE *#16*

THREAD *Yellow 6/0*

TAILS *Pale microfibbets, widely split*

DUBBING *Yellow fur or synthetic*

WINGS *Pale dun hen feathers, cut or burnt to shape*

HACKLE *Cream or pale ginger*

March Brown (left) and Sulphur Dun (right).

patterns exemplify two approaches I utilize to represent mayfly duns. The March Brown employs a reverse-palmer hackling technique in which the hackles are secured in front of the wings and wound in spaced, open-palmer style back to the bend. Most hackle feathers are slightly concave on their dull sides, and when they are affixed with concave sides facing the hook eye and wound toward the bend, the fibers in front flare forward slightly and those behind the wing angle backwards, balancing the fly perfectly without requiring tail support. A wide, inverted V is trimmed from the underside of the wound hackle, permitting the fly to float low.

In the Sulphur Dun a similar light pattern is achieved with a single hackle wound parachute-style underneath the thorax. Since tail support is not required in either of these two styles, the function of the widely split tails is purely aeronautical, helping to ensure that the fly always alights upright.

[Grayling, Michigan, U.S.A.]

Darrel Martin

The lake dimpled with rising trout. Gray duns drifted in the evening breeze while the sun crouched on the ridge. All day, a summer's sun, wafered against a hollow sky, had pressed the waters and pushed the trout deep. But now, near evening, the lake surrendered her hazy heat and her trout. Emerging gray duns, the spotted *Callibaetis*, budded on the surface and then, like living petals, blew away. Trout rings snared some from below while swallows dipped to those above.

From my fly box, I selected an Adams, and a cast placed it among the rings. As I watched the Adams nod through the expanding ribs of a ring, the rod tip plunged and bent. Line cut deeply away and whirred into the lake. A trout was on. The bent rod and stubborn line soon led the trout to net. Before me lay an enmeshed rainbow speaking silently before its release. I eased out the Adams and watched a scarlet flank fade into the water. The trout never knew that it had already been caught while the Adams was locked in my flyting vise. Even if the Adams had never taken a summer trout, there were the winter dreams.

In a way, tying is trouting. Tying extends our understanding of nature. We seek the perfect pattern, even if the perfect pattern never exists. It matters only that we seek. We seek the perfect feather, the perfect method, the perfect theory. To the thoughtful tyer, it is the quest and not the pattern that matters. And in the search, fragments of fur and feather continuously transform into a new alchemy. Part of the pleasure of tying is discovery. So, we finally net more than trout. We net knowing the spotted *Callibaetis*, the underfur of the muskrat, the scarlet flank of a rainbow and the *peent* of whispering nighthawks.

[Tacoma, Washington, U.S.A.]

GRAY MIDGE

HOOK *Partridge Roman Moser Arrow Point barbless or Partridge CS21 Sneck Midge*

SIZE *#14 to #22*

THREAD *Gray Thompson Monobond 6/0 or Taff Price Super Fine Flye-Tye*

BODY *Gray goose secondary feather barb*

WINGS *Cream or white hackle tips*

OVERWING *Havana or cream cul de canard feathers*

HACKLE *Dun, dry hackle*

Bas A. Verschoor

CINNAMON "DUTCH" ADAMS

HOOK *Partridge L3A Captain Hamilton*

SIZE *#10 to #14*

THREAD *Tan*

TAIL *Artificial fibers from a paintbrush, brown barred black*

BODY *Deerhair dyed brown, clipped and burnt to shape*

WINGS *Hackle tips from dyed grizzly neck*

HACKLE *Medium ginger and dyed grizzly*

When I look at directions for a pattern or at a finished fly, I always ask myself, "Is there any room for improvement?" Then I begin to experiment by using various alternative materials for the different parts of the fly. Sometimes there are failures, and in some cases, such as the Cinnamon "Dutch" Adams, my experiments prove to be successful. After I tie a fly, I like to be able to lean back behind my vise and say, "That is something beautiful!" If the fly catches fish as an added bonus, so much the better, and many of my flies do.

I strive to make a fly that is perfect in its proportions, and I try to find a balance between natural and artificial materials. For instance, I have solved the problem of choosing the best material for tails on dry flies by using artificial paintbrush fibers. Not only are they relatively easy and cheap to come by, but they can be dyed any color. I now use them on all my dry flies because good hackles are increasingly difficult to obtain in Europe.

My particular style of tying is a combination of American patterns flavored with Continental inventiveness. When I started tying flies, I mostly used English materials and followed English patterns that I saw in books. After gradually becoming acquainted with the American style of tying, I was greatly influenced by the advances of American tyers. Over the years, I have come to believe that in order to get the most enjoyment from fly-fishing, one should tie his or her own concoctions to fool the fish. Otherwise, the circle is not complete.

I have also concluded that fly-fishing is the right approach to fishing as a whole. Using exquisite tools—a handmade split-cane rod, a well-balanced reel, a fly line of the correct taper and a leader of the proper length—gives me infinite pleasure. When I am tying, my imagination often takes me to the stream. I carefully cast my fly upstream, see a fish rise and a small ring appear on the water, and I am in business again.

[The Hague, Netherlands]

Preben Torp Jacobsen

The long history of flytying shows that all over the world mankind has used flies to imitate nature. Fish can be caught on any fly even if it is not a masterpiece in the art of flytying, and making your own flies, however artistic they may be, can provide new insights into fly-fishing by enabling you to express your angling theories in a tangible form. For me, flytying is one of the most creative elements of fly-fishing. In tying flies, I have always strived for the greatest level of skill possible so that I could proudly present them to both man and trout.

I have been involved in many aspects of flytying. As a follower of the traditional English styles, I do not use synthetics or other recent gimmicks and have spent considerable time procuring natural materials. For three decades, I have bred my own cocks so that I can have hackles of excellent quality and in a wide range of shades. When I wrote my first book on dry-fly fishing, I learned how to make watercolors in order to convey a more accurate impression of flies and feathers than I found was possible with photography. I also drew the various stages of actual insects, which enabled me to reproduce the subtle colors that make up a fly. In doing this, I refined my knowledge of entomology, especially the changes that insects undergo throughout their life cycle.

People are fascinated by new fly patterns. Each issue of a fly-fishing magazine contains many new patterns. Rather than follow these, it is often more interesting for fly-fishers to learn about conventional flytying styles, then go out and create their own patterns. They will surely catch fish. In this world of ours, nearly everything can be bought for the right sum of money. But nothing can compare with the moment that a fly of your own making, competing with the natural, is accepted by the fish.

[Hobro, Denmark]

Claret Spinner, Hare's Face and Light Ollie (clockwise from upper left).

LIGHT OLLIE
HOOK *Mustad 72709*
SIZE *#15*
THREAD *Primrose silk*
TAIL *Buff Orpington fibers*
RIB *Silver wire*
BODY *Four strands of heron herl, dyed primrose*
HACKLES *Natural blue dun cock tied palmer style for rear hackle, light honey dun cock for front hackle*

HARE'S FACE
HOOK *Hardy, turned-up eye*
SIZE *#15*
THREAD *Hot orange silk*
TAIL *Dark honey dun cock*
RIB *Silver wire*
BODY *Dubbed fur from hare's face*
HACKLES *Three small Blue Wyandotte cock*

LITTLE CLARET SPINNER
HOOK *Mustad 72505*
SIZE *#15*
THREAD *Claret silk*
TAIL *Dun cock*
RIB *Gold wire*
BODY *One strand of condor herl, dyed brownish red*
WINGS *Hackle-point wings from dark rusty cock hackles*
HACKLES *Brown-olive and light green-olive*

The Terrestrial

Bob Mead

So many bugs, so little time. For me, however, this is a blessing. As with many things in life, constant repetition breeds boredom. Making a half-dozen flies of a single pattern at one time is about my limit.

In another time, many years ago, it was repetition that drove me from the conventional tying game into the exciting world of horse racing, gambling and smoke-filled bookie joints. For nearly a decade, I kept a nodding acquaintance with people who held varying degrees of notoriety and whose names came right out of a Damon Runyon short story.

After a while, the winning and losing, the highs and lows, the good times and not so good times all blended into a too-familiar rhythm. One day between races at Saratoga, a walking stick chanced to stroll up my leg, immediately became my captive and sparked an interest in a fresh, new type of flytying.

There is no room for boredom in the world of realistic flies. The challenge of imitating insects by finding new uses for basic, simple materials is unending. The prerequisites, once the fundamentals of conventional tying have been mastered, are simple patience and an inquiring mind. I have often stared at a feather or a piece of material for hours—turning, crimping, folding and snipping until something clicks. Nothing gets thrown away without critical inspection.

Most of my flies take one to four hours to tie, a few twice that long. It is not the actual tying but, rather, the preparation of individual parts that devours time. For instance, there are ten separate steps and eight individual tying procedures in the creation of a single front leg for my Praying Mantis.

Tip? When tying, keep your brain as agile as your fingers. When fishing, release a few fish. What if it turns out God is a trout?

[Scotia, New York, U.S.A.]

PRAYING MANTIS

HOOK *Partridge D4A*

SIZE *#8*

THREAD *Olive and light brown 6/0*

UNDERBODY *Quill or plastic form cut to shape of a baseball bat*

BODY *Swannundaze*

WINGS AND NECK *Olive goose wing quill*

LEGS *Green and brown goose biots tied over both sides of crimped stripped hackle stems*

EYES *Melted monofilament*

ANTENNAE *Fine deburred tips of peacock herl*

HOPPER

HOOK *Tiemco 101*

SIZE *#10 and #16*

THREAD *White 6/0*

DETACHED BODY, LEGS AND HEAD
Polypropylene yarn

FRONT AND MIDDLE LEGS
30-lb-test Dacron backing

HIND PART OF LEGS
30-lb-test Dacron backing

THORAX *Furry foam*

WINGS *Vinyl shower curtain*

ANTENNAE *12-lb-test Dacron backing*

EYES *Glass beads*

COLOR *Design Marker*

John Betts

In Europe, where our traditions originated, tied lures that looked like insects were called "flyes." Those that did not were called "lures" and they included streamers. To an extent, this distinction still exists today. Salmon flies seem to be in a category all their own and were probably called flies because by then that term, due to the procedures involved, had come into common use. In all, this system seems to be a sensible and natural one.

Throughout their history, flies and fly-tying have been born in the current of change. Indeed, if there is a continuous thread or dynamic tradition, it may be just that. If legitimate change can be called tradition, then whatever is done is a direct descendant of uninterrupted history. Changing flies encompasses more than the simple act performed on the stream and is the only way I know of to move on to something else. In my experience, anyone who limits his life to the past may miss much of what is coming.

[Denver, Colorado, U.S.A.]

Darwin Atkin

With the first fly I tied, in late 1959, in my senior year in college, I knew I had found an activity that would stay with me over a lifetime. Flytying began to consume me, and as I developed a talent for tying flies, I was invited various places to demonstrate my tying. This forced me to deal with some aspects of myself. I was very shy, and it was difficult for me to talk with people I did not know. By meeting people through my flytying, I gradually learned to break out of my shell. It has turned into the greatest thing I could have become involved with.

Based on my experience, my message to others is that you can have a lifetime love affair with flytying and fly-fishing that can take you to places you have never been and introduce you to some of the greatest people you would ever want to meet.

The Black and Tan Field Crickets symbolize how I view my life as a flytyer. Someone remarked to me that the crickets appear to be sophisticated and rather involved to make. But they are really nothing more than the results of well-thought-out basic flytying steps, applied one after the other. That is how I view all of my tying. I try to use my materials with intelligence and never forget the basic steps. One other thing about these crickets: they are really caricatures of the real insects and always keep me laughing as I tie them.

[Porterville, California, U.S.A.]

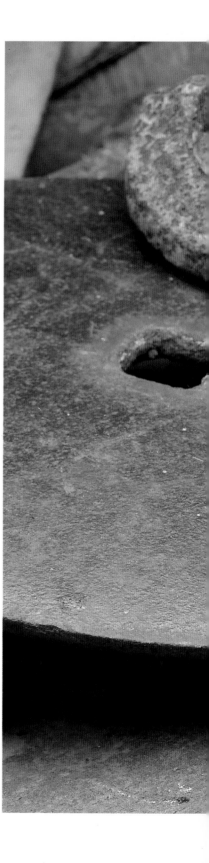

BLACK FIELD CRICKET

TAN FIELD CRICKET

HOOK *Mustad 9672*
SIZE *#6, or for particular conditions*
THREAD *Black or tan 6/0*
TAIL-END *Two lengths of 6- to 8-lb-test monofilament for body spikes, stripped hackle feather for ovipositor*
BODY *Open-cell urethane foam (Art Foam or Fun Foam) for slow-sink style, Evazote for floating style, black or tan*
UNDERWING *Black or tan deer hair*
LEGS *Ringneck pheasant tail fibers, knotted*
WING *Black or tan Microweb*
ANTENNAE *2-lb-test monofilament*
HEAD *Black or tan deer hair*

Gary LaFontaine

FLEX-HOPPER

HOOK *LaFontaine Flex-Hook*

SIZE *#2 to #8*

THREAD *Green*

BODY *Dubbed sparkle yarn, a mix of green, yellow and brown variations*

BODY HACKLE *Light ginger, palmered and clipped*

UNDERWING *Yellow and brown deer hair*

OVERWING *Turkey feather*

HEAD *Painted cork or spun and clipped deer hair*

A trout is not an intelligent creature, blessed as it is with a brain the size of a pea. My favorite description of fly-fishing comes from a friend: "a battle of wits against the unarmed."

Then what protects trout from our offerings of fur, feather and steel? A wonderful set of instincts. They feed selectively during an insect hatch, refusing everything except the prevalent food item, not because of intelligence, but because a rigid selection process protects them from mistakes. Selectivity? Trout do not select; they instinctively forfeit choice when they are locked into a feeding pattern. When this occurs, they will only take a fly that closely resembles the natural.

This causes the problems that make fly-fishing a fascinating game. For me, the act of creating a fly means first identifying one of those specific problems. When I began to research grasshoppers, I was satisfied with the popular and creative hopper imitations, especially the Dave's Hopper, Gartside Hopper and Letort Hopper, and did not intend to devise something new just for the sake of newness.

I set up an observation blind over the Clark Fork, the stream that winds through the town where I live, and tossed both natural and imitation grasshoppers into a pool full of brown trout to watch how fish fed on hoppers. Then I noticed the discrepancy. It was the first plop of the hopper onto the surface of the water that was so important. If it alerted the fish—either making the fish move toward the insect or tilt upward to wait for it—any of the good patterns worked. If the hopper landed unnoticed and drifted down over the fish, the patterns failed half the time.

There is an axiom in flytying that the larger the food item, the harder it is to imi-

Reference and Resource

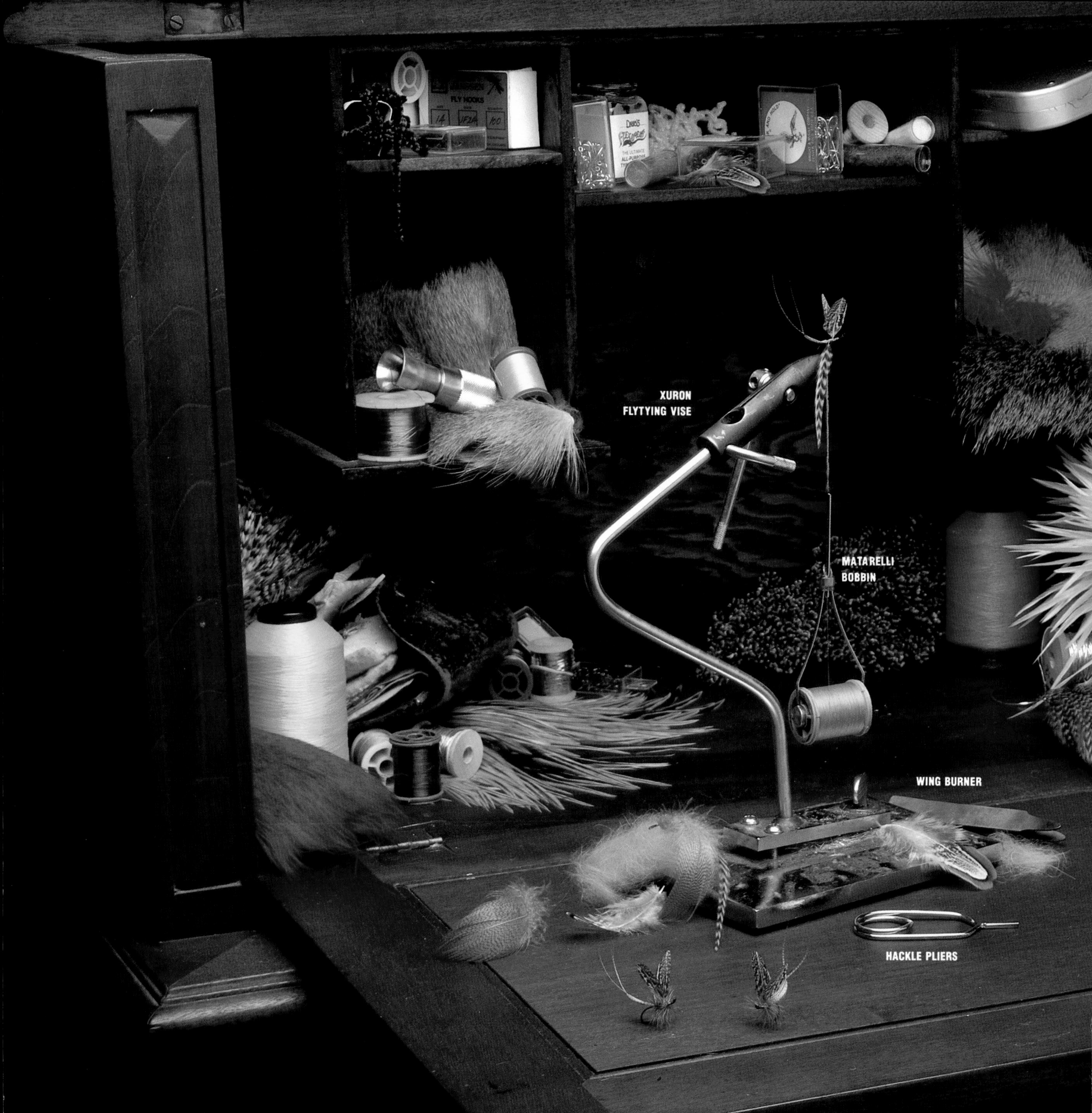

XURON
FLYTYING VISE

MATARELLI
BOBBIN

WING BURNER

HACKLE PLIERS

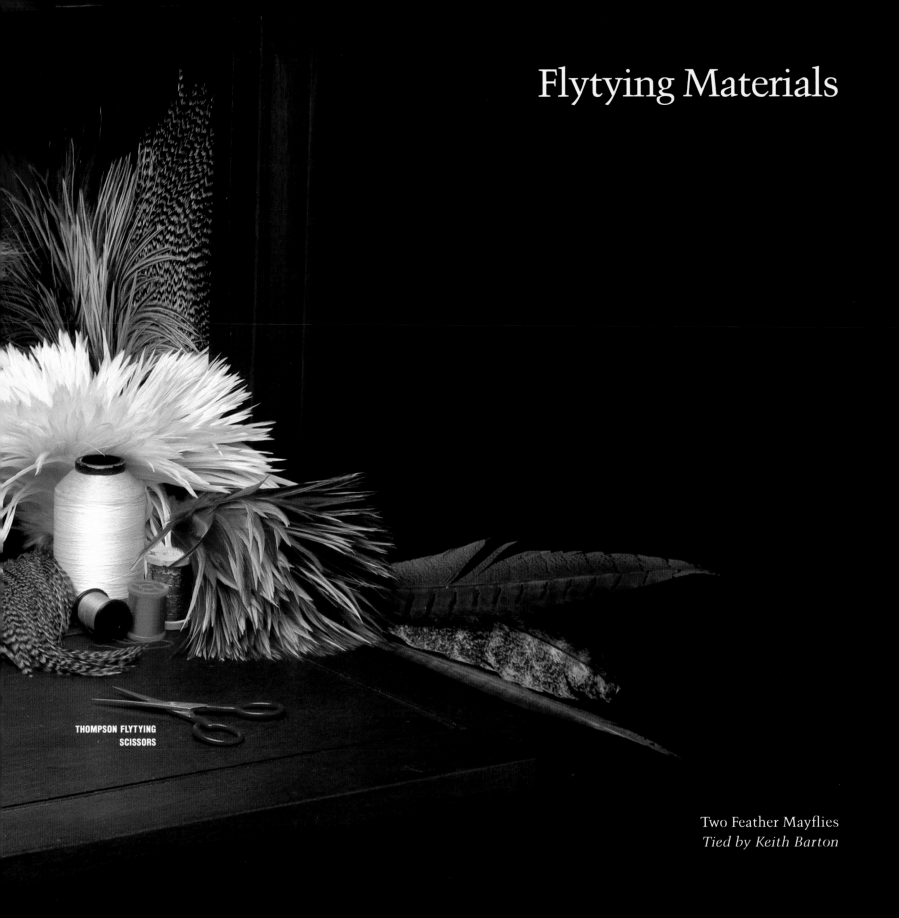

Flytying Materials

Two Feather Mayflies
Tied by Keith Barton

THOMPSON FLYTYING
SCISSORS

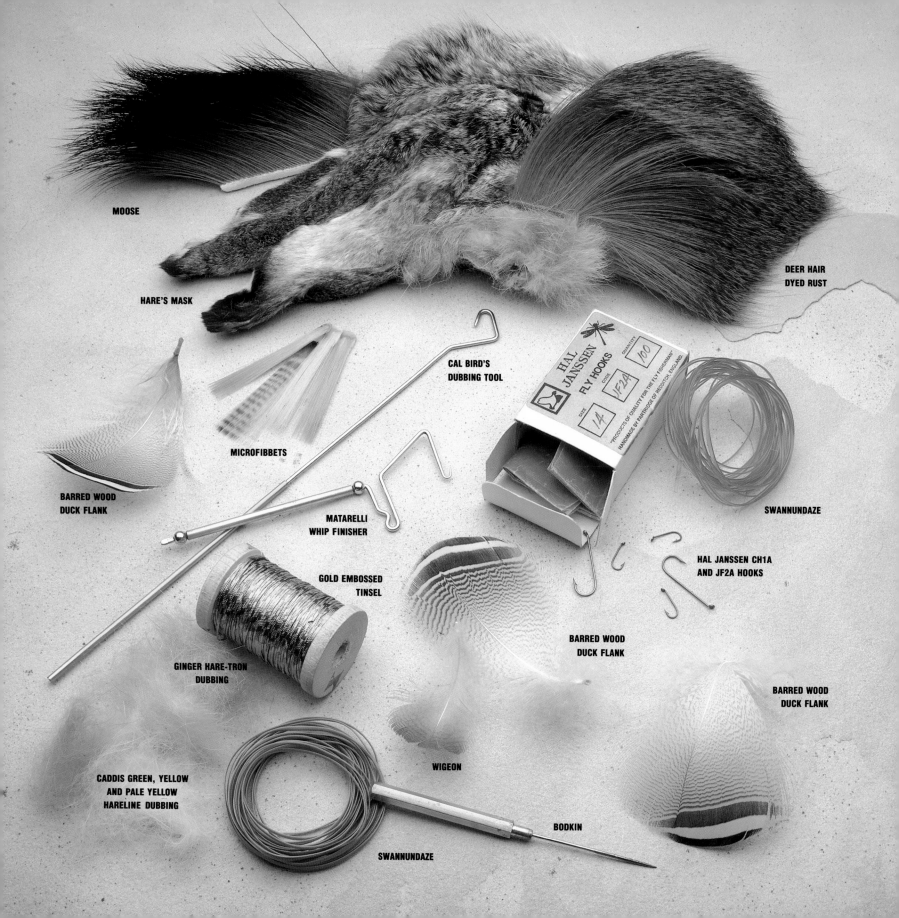

MOOSE

HARE'S MASK

DEER HAIR
DYED RUST

CAL BIRD'S
DUBBING TOOL

MICROFIBBETS

BARRED WOOD
DUCK FLANK

MATARELLI
WHIP FINISHER

SWANNUNDAZE

HAL JANSSEN CH1A
AND JF2A HOOKS

GOLD EMBOSSED
TINSEL

BARRED WOOD
DUCK FLANK

GINGER HARE-TRON
DUBBING

BARRED WOOD
DUCK FLANK

WIGEON

CADDIS GREEN, YELLOW
AND PALE YELLOW
HARELINE DUBBING

BODKIN

SWANNUNDAZE

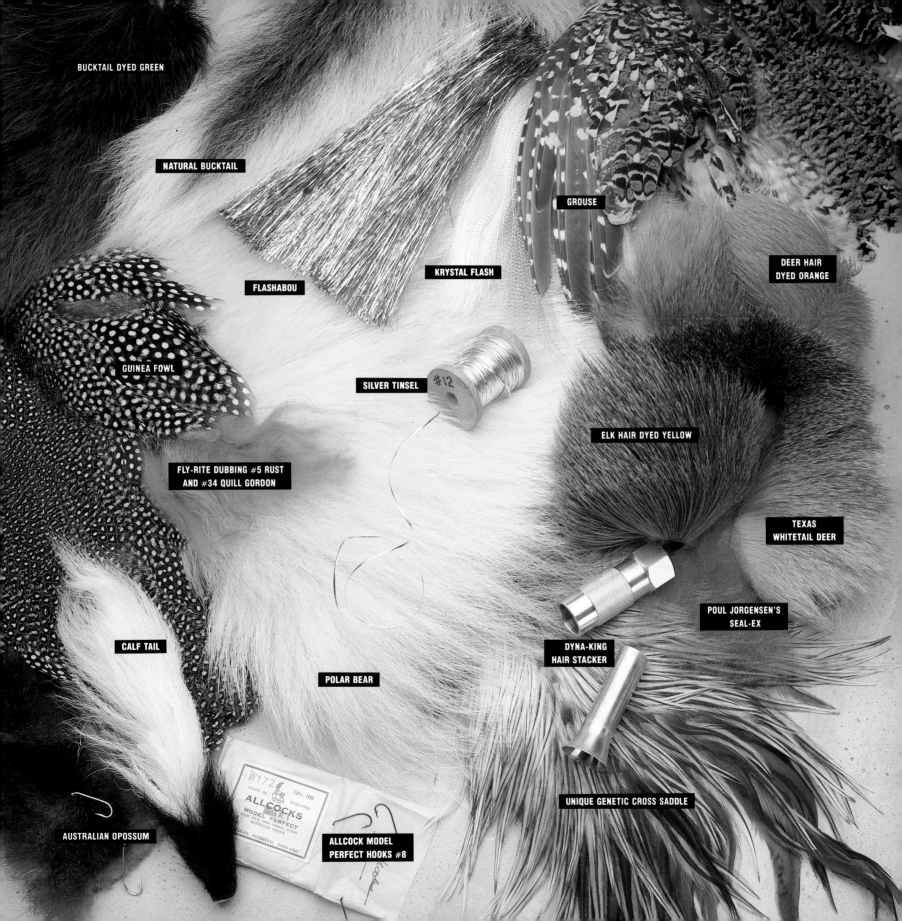

BUCKTAIL DYED GREEN

NATURAL BUCKTAIL

GROUSE

DEER HAIR
DYED ORANGE

KRYSTAL FLASH

FLASHABOU

GUINEA FOWL

SILVER TINSEL

ELK HAIR DYED YELLOW

FLY-RITE DUBBING #5 RUST
AND #34 QUILL GORDON

TEXAS
WHITETAIL DEER

POUL JORGENSEN'S
SEAL-EX

CALF TAIL

DYNA-KING
HAIR STACKER

POLAR BEAR

UNIQUE GENETIC CROSS SADDLE

AUSTRALIAN OPOSSUM

ALLCOCK MODEL
PERFECT HOOKS #8

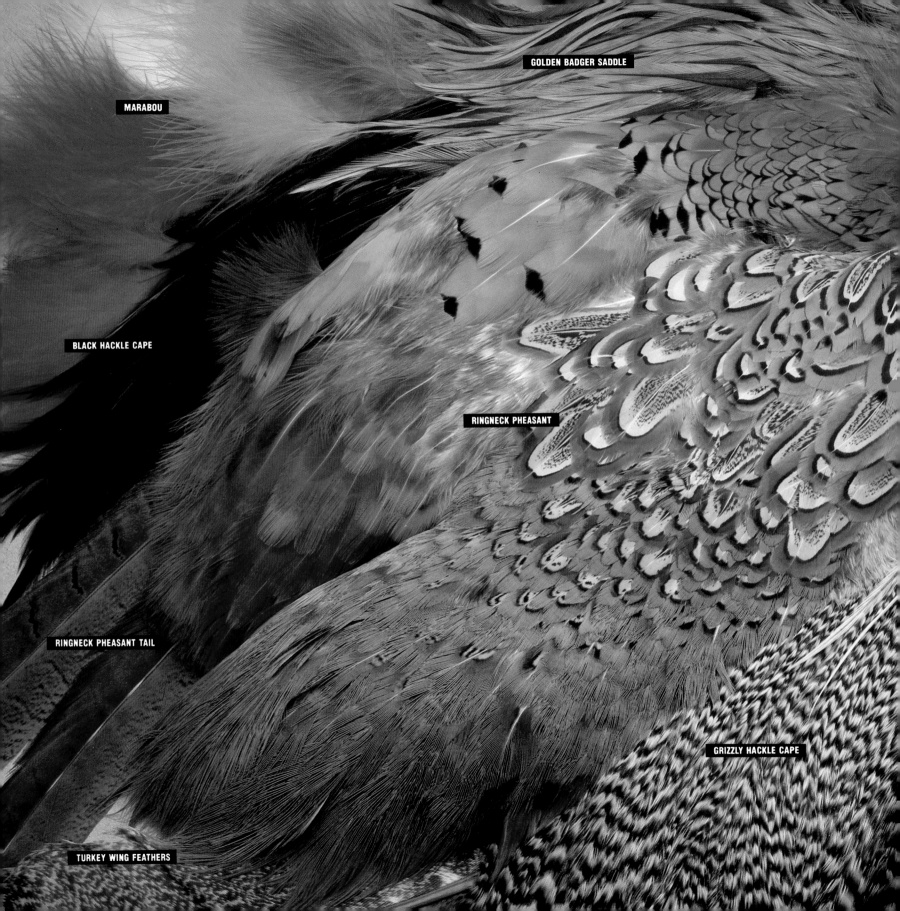

Trout Flies to Scale

By Page Number and Hook Size

Flytyer's Library

This bibliography lists books by flytyers in *The Art of the Trout Fly* that are out of print as well as current editions. All books are in hardcover unless otherwise noted. Also included are video- and audiotapes.

Betts, John

Synthetic Flies. Red Bank, New Jersey: self-published, 1980 (softcover). Out of print.

Flies with an "Edited Hackle." Red Bank, New Jersey: self-published, 1982 (softcover).

Borger, Gary

Nymphing, A Basic Book. Harrisburg, Pennsylvania: Stackpole, 1979.

Naturals: A Guide to Food Organisms of the Trout. Harrisburg, Pennsylvania: Stackpole, 1980.

"Nymphing with Gary Borger," videotape. Wausau, Wisconsin: Borger Films, Ltd., 1982.

"Fishing the Dry Fly," videotape. St. Paul, Minnesota: Scientific Anglers/3M, 1983.

"Fly Fishing for Trout," videotape. St. Paul, Minnesota: Scientific Anglers/3M, 1983.

"Tying Trout Flies," videotape. St. Paul, Minnesota: Scientific Anglers/3M, 1983.

"The Fabulous Big Horn," videotape. Wausau, Wisconsin: Borger Films, Ltd., 1986.

"South Island Sampler," videotape. Wausau, Wisconsin: Borger Films, Ltd., 1986.

"Bow River Adventure," videotape. Wausau, Wisconsin: Borger Films, Ltd., 1987.

"Trout in Stillwaters," videotape. Wausau, Wisconsin: Borger Films, Ltd., 1987.

Boyle, Robert H.

Sport, Mirror of American Life. Boston: Little Brown, 1963. Out of print.

The Hudson River, A Natural and Unnatural History. New York: W. W. Norton, 1969.

The Hudson River, A Natural and Unnatural History. New York: Norton Library, 1979 (enlarged edition).

Malignant Neglect (with the Environmental Defense Fund). New York: Alfred A. Knopf, 1979.

Malignant Neglect. New York: Vintage Books, 1980 (softcover).

At the Top of Their Game. New York: Nick Lyons Books, 1983.

Boyle, Robert H., and Boyle, R. Alexander

Acid Rain. New York: Nick Lyons Books/Schocken Books, 1983.

Boyle, Robert H., and Ciampi, Elgin (photographs)

Bass. New York: W. W. Norton, 1980.

Boyle, Robert H., Graves, John, and Watkins, T. H.

The Water Hustlers. New York and San Francisco: Sierra Club, 1971. Out of print.

Boyle, Robert H., and Leiser, Eric

Stoneflies for the Angler. New York: Alfred A. Knopf, 1982.

Boyle, Robert H., and Whitlock, Dave, editors

The Fly Tyer's Almanac. New York: Crown Publishers, 1975.

The Second Fly-Tyer's Almanac. Philadelphia and New York: J. B. Lippincott, 1978. Out of print.

The Fly Tyer's Almanac. New York: Nick Lyons Books, 1983 (softcover).

Davy, Alf

The "Gilly," A Flyfisher's Guide. Kelowna, British Columbia: self-published, 1985.

The "Gilly," A Flyfisher's Guide. Kelowna, British Columbia: self-published, 1987 (softcover).

Goddard, John

Trout Fly Recognition. London: A. & C. Black, 1966, 1974. Out of print.

Trout Flies of Stillwater. London: A. & C. Black, 1969, 1972, 1975. Out of print.

Trout Fly Recognition. London: A. & C. Black, 1976.

Big Fish from Salt Water. London: Ernest Benn, 1977. Out of print.

The Super Flies of Stillwater. London: Ernest Benn,

1977. Out of print.

Trout Flies of Stillwater. London: A. & C. Black, 1979.

Stillwater Flies, How and When to Fish Them. London: Ernest Benn, 1982. Out of print.

The Super Flies of Stillwater. London: A. & C. Black, 1982.

Stillwater Flies, How and When to Fish Them. London: A. & C. Black, 1985.

John Goddard's Waterside Guide. London: Unwin Hyman, 1988.

Goddard, John, and Clarke, Brian

The Trout and the Fly. London: Ernest Benn, 1980, 1981. Out of print.

The Trout and the Fly. New York: Nick Lyons Books/ Doubleday, 1980. Out of print.

The Trout and the Fly. New York: Nick Lyons Books, 1980 (softcover).

The Trout and the Fly. London: A. & C. Black, 1984.

Grant, George F.

The Art of Weaving Hair Hackles for Trout Flies. Butte, Montana: self-published, 1971 (softcover). Out of print.

Montana Trout Flies. Butte, Montana: self-published, 1972 (softcover). Out of print.

The Master Fly Weaver. Portland, Oregon: Champoeg Press, 1980.

Montana Trout Flies. Portland, Oregon: Champoeg Press, 1981.

Jacobsen, Preben Torp

Tørfluefiskeri (Dry-Fly Fishing). Copenhagen: Grafisk Forlag, 1965 (softcover; in Danish). Out of print.

Nymfefiskeri (Nymph Fishing). Hobro, Denmark: Flyleaves, 1972 (softcover; in Danish).

Fluebinding (Fly-Tying). Hobro, Denmark: Flyleaves, 1976 (softcover; in Danish).

Fluer, Fisk & Fiskere (Flies, Fish & Fishermen). Hobro, Denmark: Flyleaves, 1977 (in Danish).

Tørfluefiskeri—Fluefiskeri paa, i og lige under vandoverfladen (Dryfly-Fishing—Flyfishing on, in and just under the surface). Hobro, Denmark: Flyleaves, 1978 (softcover; in Danish).

Stangbygning, Bygning af splitcane-fluestaenger (Rodbuilding, Building of splitcane-flyrods). Hobro, Denmark: Flyleaves, 1982 (in Danish).

El Manuscrito de Astorga. Juan de Bergara. Año 1624 (The Manuscript of Astorga). Hobro, Denmark: Flyleaves, 1984 (softcover; in Spanish, French and English).

Janssen, Hal

"Hal Janssen's Fly Fishing Secrets," videotapes. Santa Rosa, California: Sonoma Video Productions.—
"The Dry Fly," 1982.
"The Wet Fly and Nymph," 1982.
"Advance Fishing Techniques—The Mayfly," 1983.

Jorgensen, Poul

Dressing Flies for Fresh and Salt Water. Rockville Centre, New York: Freshet Press, 1973. Out of print.

Modern Fly Dressings for the Practical Angler. New York: Winchester Press, 1976.

Salmon Flies: Their Character, Style, and Dressing. Harrisburg, Pennsylvania: Stackpole, 1978.

Modern Trout Flies and How to Tie Them. New York: Nick Lyons Books/Doubleday, 1979 (hard- and softcover).

Modern Trout Flies and How to Tie Them. New York: Nick Lyons Books/Winchester Press, 1984 (softcover).

Kaufmann, Randall

American Nymph Fly Tying Manual. Portland, Oregon: Frank Amato Publications, 1975 (hard- and softcover).

The Fly Tyers Nymph Manual. Portland, Oregon: Western Fisherman's Press, 1986 (hard- and softcover).

Kaufmann, Randall, and Cordes, Ron

Lake Fishing with a Fly. Portland, Oregon: Frank Amato Publications, 1985 (hard- and softcover).

LaFontaine, Gary

Challenge of the Trout. Missoula, Montana: Mountain Press Publishing Company, 1976. Out of print.

Caddisflies. New York: Nick Lyons Books/Winchester

Press, 1983.

Fly Fishing Mysteries. Helena, Montana: Greycliff Publishing Co., 1988.

"River Rap Series," audiotape interviews. Helena, Montana: Greycliff Publishing Co.—
Craig Mathews. "Fly Fishing the Madison River," 1986.
Bob Jacklin. "Fly Fishing the Upper Yellowstone," 1987.
Mike Lawson. "Fly Fishing the Henry's Fork," 1987.
Anderson, George. "Fly Fishing the Spring Creeks of the Paradise Valley," 1988.
John Bailey. "Fly Fishing the Middle Yellowstone," 1988.
Eric Peper. "Fly Fishing the Beaverkill," 1988.
Dale Spartas. "Fly Fishing the Housatonic," 1988.

LaFontaine, Gary, and Dennis, Jack

"Tying and Fishing Caddisflies," videotape. Jackson, Wyoming: Snake River Books, 1988.

Lively, Chauncy K.

Chauncy Lively's Flybox: A Portfolio of Modern Trout Flies. Harrisburg, Pennsylvania: Stackpole, 1980 (softcover).

Martin, Darrel

Imitations: Methods in Tying and Trouting. Seattle, Washington: Sun King Publishing, 1980 (softcover). Out of print.

The Fly Tyer's Sketchbook. Seattle, Washington: Sun King Publishing, 1981 (softcover). Out of print.

The Waterlogue: A Fly Fisher's Workbook. Seattle, Washington: Sun King Publishing, 1981 (softcover). Out of print.

Fly-Tying Methods. New York: Nick Lyons Books, 1987.

McDowell, Hugh

New Zealand Fly-Tying, The ten-thumbed beginner's guide. Auckland, New Zealand: Reed Methuen, 1984 (softcover).

Moser, Roman

"Effective Flytying," videotape. Siegsdorf, West Germany: Traun River Products, 1987 (in German).

"Fishing the Sedge Fly," videotape. Rijswijk, Netherlands: AMR Video Productions, 1988 (German and English versions).

Rosborough, E. H. "Polly"

Tying and Fishing the Fuzzy Nymphs. Chiloquin, Oregon: self-published, 1965 (softcover). Out of print.

Tying and Fishing the Fuzzy Nymphs. Manchester, Vermont: Orvis, 1969. Out of print.

Tying and Fishing the Fuzzy Nymphs. Harrisburg, Pennsylvania: Stackpole, 1979. Out of print.

Reminiscences From 50 Years of Flyrodding. Chiloquin, Oregon: self-published, 1982. Out of print.

Tying and Fishing the Fuzzy Nymphs. Harrisburg, Pennsylvania: Stackpole, 1988.

"Polly Rosborough Ties His Fuzzy Nymphs, Part I," videotape. Ashland, Oregon: Pegasus Productions, 1988.

Shaw, Helen

Fly-Tying. New York: Ronald Press Company, 1963. Out of print.

Fly-Tying. New York: John Wiley and Sons, 1980. Out of print.

Fly-Tying. New York: John Wiley and Sons, 1983 (softcover). Out of print.

Fly-Tying. New York: Nick Lyons Books, 1987 (twenty-fifth anniversary edition).

Talleur, Richard W.

Fly Fishing for Trout: A Guide for Adult Beginners. New York: Winchester Press, 1974. Out of print.

Mastering the Art of Fly Tying. Harrisburg, Pennsylvania: Stackpole, 1979.

The Fly Tyer's Primer. New York: Nick Lyons Books/ Winchester Press, 1986.

Fly Fishing for Trout: A Guide for Beginners. Piscataway, New Jersey: Winchester Press, 1987.

The Fly Tyer's Primer. New York: Nick Lyons Books, 1988 (softcover).

Tashiro, Nori, and Tashiro, Tada

The Tashiro Nymphs and the Naturals. Tokyo: Tiemco,

1981 (in Japanese).

The World of the Tashiro Nymphs. Tokyo: Tiemco, 1986 (in Japanese).

Whitlock, Dave

Dave Whitlock's Guide to Aquatic Trout Foods. New York: Nick Lyons Books/Winchester Press, 1982.

L. L. Bean Fly-Fishing Handbook. New York: Nick Lyons Books/Winchester Press, 1983 (softcover).

L. L. Bean's Fly Fishing for Bass Handbook. New York: Nick Lyons Books, 1988 (softcover).

See also Boyle, Robert H.

"Fly Fishing for Bass with Dave Whitlock," videotape. Fort Worth, Texas: Sport's Tapes, 1986.

"Introduction to Fly Fishing," videotape. Freeport, Maine: L. L. Bean, 1986.

Wulff, Lee

Lee Wulff's Handbook of Fresh Water Fishing. New York: Frederick A. Stokes, 1939. Out of print.

Let's Go Fishing! Philadelphia and New York: J. B. Lippincott, 1939. Out of print.

Leaping Silver. New York: George W. Stewart, 1940. Out of print.

Sports Photography. New York: A. S. Barnes, 1942. Out of print.

Lee Wulff's New Handbook of Fresh Water Fishing. Philadelphia and New York: J. B. Lippincott, 1951. Out of print.

The Atlantic Salmon. New York: A. S. Barnes, 1958. Out of print.

The Sportsman's Companion. New York: Harper & Row, 1968. Out of print.

Fishing with Lee Wulff. New York: Alfred A. Knopf, 1972.

Lee Wulff on Flies. Harrisburg, Pennsylvania: Stackpole, 1980.

The Atlantic Salmon. New York: Nick Lyons Books/Winchester Press, 1983.

Lee Wulff on Flies. Harrisburg, Pennsylvania: Stackpole, 1985 (softcover).

Trout on a Fly. New York: Nick Lyons Books, 1986 (hardcover and deluxe editions).

Flytyer's Address Book and Index

Darwin Atkin (108)
354 North York Street
Porterville, California
93257
U.S.A.

Keith Barton (116)
1000 Ashbury Street #2
San Francisco, California
94117
U.S.A.

**Barry and
Cathy Beck** (23)
Fishing Creek Outfitters
RR 1, Raven Creek Road
Benton, Pennsylvania 17814
U.S.A.

John Betts (107)
1452 South Elizabeth
Denver, Colorado 80210
U.S.A.

Calvert T. Bird (18)
2380 Van Buren Court
Reno, Nevada 89503
U.S.A.

Bill Blackstone (26)
2740 Bennett Avenue
Orange, California 92669
U.S.A.

Gary Borger (68)
Gary Borger Enterprises
PO Box 628
Wausau, Wisconsin 54402
U.S.A.

Robert H. Boyle (34)
Lane Gate Road
Cold Spring, New York
10516
U.S.A.

Alf Davy (72)
PO Box 1738
Kelowna, British Columbia
V1Y 8M3
Canada

**Walt, Winnie and
Mary Dette** (90)
Dette Trout Flies
Roscoe, New York 12776
U.S.A.

Tim England (63)
PO Box 40
Bellvue, Colorado 80512
U.S.A.

Jack Gartside (38)
10 Sachem Street
Boston, Massachusetts
02120
U.S.A.

John Goddard (47)
Plymtree
Seven Hills Road
Cobham, Surrey
England

George F. Grant (71)
PO Box 3142
Butte, Montana 59702
U.S.A.

**René and Bonnie
Harrop** (21)
PO Box 491
St. Anthony, Idaho 83445
U.S.A.

**Preben Torp
Jacobsen** (100)
Flyleaves
Søndermarksvej 116
Hvilsom
DK-9500 Hobro
Denmark

Hal Janssen (48)
Hal Janssen Company
PO Box 11491
Santa Rosa, California
95406
U.S.A.

Poul Jorgensen (67)
PO Box 382
Cottage Street
Roscoe, New York 12776
U.S.A.

Randall Kaufmann (64)
Streamborn Flies
PO Box 23032
Portland, Oregon 97223
U.S.A.

Gary LaFontaine (111)
PO Box 166
Deer Lodge, Montana 58722
U.S.A.

Chauncy K. Lively (93)
Route 3, Box 3292-B
Grayling, Michigan 49738
U.S.A.

Darrel Martin (96)
7410 Forty-eighth
Avenue East
Tacoma, Washington 98443
U.S.A.

Hugh McDowell (37)
Angling Adventures
PO Box 297
Ngongotaha, Rotorua
New Zealand

Robert McHaffie (51)
33 Glengiven Avenue
Limavady,
County Londonderry
Northern Ireland

Dave McNeese (29)
1191 Third Street NW
Salem, Oregon 97304
U.S.A.

Bob Mead (104)
27 Harmon Road
Scotia, New York 12302
U.S.A.

**R. Monty
Montplaisir** (44)
PO Box 23
Averill, Vermont 05901
U.S.A.

Roman Moser (86)
Kuferzeile 19
4810 Gmunden
Austria

Neil Patterson (80)
Wilderness Lodge
Little Wawcott
Elcot Turn, Bath Road
Newbury, Berkshire
England

André Puyans (83)
170 Sierra Drive, #7
Walnut Creek, California
94596
U.S.A.

**E. H. "Polly"
Rosborough** (52)
PO Box 36
Chiloquin, Oregon 97624
U.S.A.

Paul Schmookler (55)
35 Irving Street
Millis, Massachusetts 02054
U.S.A.

Helen Shaw (79)
c/o Nick Lyons Books
31 West Twenty-first Street
New York, New York 10010
U.S.A.

Richard W. Talleur (56)
47-C Friars' Gate
Clifton Park, New York
12065
U.S.A.

Nori Tashiro (41)
3-20-3 Kaminagaya
Konan-Ku, Yokohama
Japan 233

Tada Tashiro (41)
3-15-17 Kaminagaya
Konan-Ku, Yokohama
Japan 233

Al Troth (76)
PO Box 1307
Dillon, Montana 59725
U.S.A.

Bas A. Verschoor (99)
80 Brasemdaal
2553 NG The Hague
Netherlands

Dave Whitlock (59)
c/o L. L. Bean
Freeport, Maine 04033
U.S.A.

Lee Wulff (89)
Lee Wulff Productions
Beaverkill Road
Lew Beach, New York 12753
U.S.A.